CRASH AT CORONA

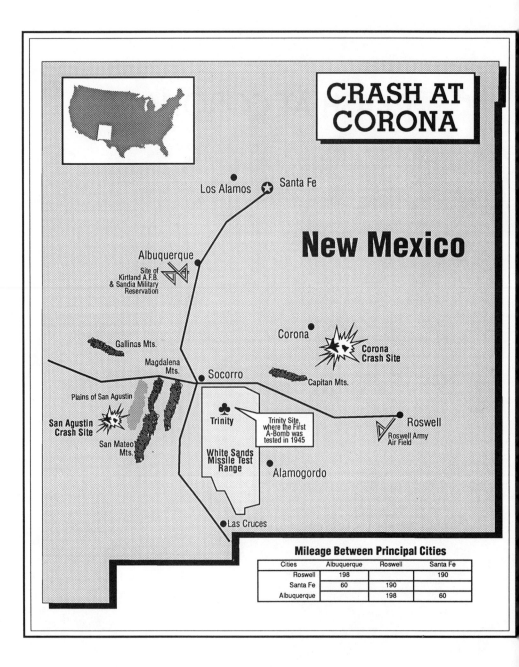

CRASH AT CORONA

New Mexico

Los Alamos • ✪ Santa Fe

Albuquerque •
Site of
Kirtland A.F.B.
& Sandia Military
Reservation

Gallinas Mts.

Corona •

Corona
Crash Site

Magdalena
Mts.

Socorro •

Capitan Mts.

Plains of San Agustin

**San Agustin
Crash Site**

San Mateo
Mts.

Trinity

Trinity Site,
where the First
A-Bomb was
tested in 1945

• Roswell
Roswell Army
Air Field

White Sands
Missile Test
Range

Alamogordo •

• Las Cruces

Mileage Between Principal Cities

Cities	Albuquerque	Roswell	Santa Fe
Roswell	198		190
Santa Fe	60	190	
Albuquerque		198	60

CRASH AT CORONA

THE U.S. MILITARY RETRIEVAL AND COVER-UP OF A UFO

Stanton T. Friedman & Don Berliner

PARAGON HOUSE

NEW YORK

First edition, 1992

Published in the United States by

Paragon House
90 Fifth Avenue
New York, NY 10011

Library of Congress Cataloging-in-Publication Data

Friedman, Stanton T.
    Crash at Corona : the U.S. military retrieval and cover-up of a
UFO / Stanton T. Friedman & Don Berliner.—1st ed.
        p.   cm.
    Includes bibliographical references and index.
    ISBN 1-55778-449-3
    1. Unidentified flying objects—Sightings and encounters—New
Mexico—Corona.   I. Berliner, Don.   II. Title.
[TL789.3.F75   1992]
001.9'42—dc20   92-10176
                                                                CIP

Manufactured in the United States of America

Frontispiece by Landon Wickham.

Contents

Acknowledgments

THE AUTHORS WISH to express their sincere gratitude to the Fund for UFO Research and Robert Bigelow for their moral and financial support, to the hundreds of people to whom we've talked about various aspects of the crashed saucer problem, to the Mutual UFO Network for publishing so many papers about crashed saucers, to *Unsolved Mysteries* for its outstanding production about crashed UFOs in New Mexico, and to their agent John White and their editor Andy DeSalvo. Special thanks to Gerald Anderson, John Carpenter, Glenn Dennis, Walter Haut, Alice Knight, Vern Maltais, Dr. Jesse Marcel, Sappho Henderson, Loretta Proctor, Robert Porter, Phyllis McGuire, Elizabeth Tulk, Barbara Dugger, Robert Shirkey, L. W. Rickett, General Thomas Jefferson DuBose, Jack Tiffany, researcher Renneta Friesen, and many more for their cooperation, time, and trust in us.

Stanton Friedman wishes to express special gratitude to his family for putting up with his obsession with crashed saucers and his many weeks away from home for more than a decade before finally co-authoring this long talked-of book.

Preface

REDUCED TO ITS SIMPLEST TERMS, this is a book to answer one of the most common questions about UFOs: If they are real, why hasn't one ever crashed? The underlying implication is that since UFOs presumably don't crash, they must not be real.

The study of thousands of reports from excellent observers (airline pilots, military pilots) of close-range, daylight observations of apparently manufactured craft whose shapes and performance defy even the latest of scientific theories certainly supports the contention that some of the things reported as UFOs are almost certainly real—and completely unexplained.

The lack of solid evidence that even one had crashed had bothered serious students of the subject for decades. It was hard to imagine that any constructed devices could be so flawless that they never failed. And without something more than an untraceable rumor of a crash, it was difficult to make much of a case for UFO reality, let alone alien origin.

The need for an improved, updated, more understandable and more readable book to follow the 1980 *Roswell Incident* by Bill Moore and Charles Berlitz had been on the mind of lecturer/researcher Stanton Friedman for many years. Having done much of the investigating for that book, he continued to dig into the crash near Corona, New Mexico. (Nothing crashed at Roswell, despite the titles of books; it was just the largest city within seventy-five miles of the crash site.) Stan spent years tracking down witnesses and widows of witnesses and neighbors and co-workers and anyone else who might be able to add even a tiny scrap to the slowly jelling story.

A plan to co-write a follow-up book with Bill Moore came to naught, but the idea and the pressing need remained. Steadily, the information and the confirmations of earlier information were piling up, and so any subsequent book would undoubtedly be stronger and more convincing. Through the 1980s, however, Friedman's only outlet for the story he was gathering through hundreds of phone calls monthly and thousands of miles of travel were formal papers (some written with Moore) published privately or presented at MUFON (Mutual UFO Network) annual conferences.

In the summer of 1989, he persuaded the producers of the NBC-TV series *Unsolved Mysteries* to do a major investigative segment on the Corona crash and served as a technical adviser to the show, which led off the 1989 fall season. The intense audience reaction to the original airing in September 1989 and to the rerun in January 1990 surprised everyone but Friedman. Scores of viewers called a special telephone number to record their involvement (direct, indirect, through hearsay, or imaginary) in some aspect of the mysterious events in New Mexico. This produced quite a few interesting leads, which in turn revealed a few previously unsuspected sources of valuable information. This was especially true of the lesser-known crash at the Plains of San Agustin, where a firsthand witness came forward.

In 1989, Friedman proposed a book about the new evidence for the Corona and San Agustin crashes to literary agent John White. At about the same time, aviation/science writer Don Berliner offered a similar idea to White, who had previously found him a publisher for an aviation book. White brought them together and suggested they collaborate, with Friedman concentrating on the investigation and Berliner on the writing.

The two had already worked together when Friedman's proposed investigation of the highly controversial Majestic-12 documents was financed in 1988 by the Fund for UFO Research, on whose executive committee Berliner sat. They had long been acquainted and each considered the other to be among the small group in the private UFO community whose work could be counted upon. In mid-1990, following a private conference of crash witnesses sponsored by the fund, a contract was signed and research and writing accelerated.

The search for proof of the crash of even one UFO has been a long string of frustrations punctuated by the occasional joyful discovery of a witness whose story checked out and whose background was solid. But most leads turned out to be nothing or simply couldn't be checked out at all. One woman who claimed her father had been a military doctor who performed an autopsy on an alien body was revealed to have a disturbingly active imagination, according to members of her family.

Friedman was determined to follow a strict scientific method, so he began the painstaking search through voluminous records, and files, and old newspapers. Other UFO investigators had grabbed vague rumors and built them into wonderfully detailed stories that had no basis in fact. Still others had apparently invented tales to satisfy the insatiable hunger of the press and the public for answers to questions that remain unanswered.

Each such episode, whether exposed by members of the private UFO community or by extremists in the anti-UFO clique, hurt those who were patiently sifting a mountain of sand in hope of finding a flake of gold. But enough shiny specks were found to keep the serious searchers sifting ever more sand in the hope of finding the mother lode. And even though some carefully planted "fool's gold" turned up, the real stuff was there, too. Not the absolute proof that everyone wanted—demanded—but an encouraging collection of intriguing bits.

One of the major handicaps Friedman faced was the antiquity of the event. Those who had held important positions when the crashes occurred—generals, legislators, cabinet members, scientists—were, with rare exceptions, long dead. All the people who had known more than a small portion of the huge story were gone, and their memoirs were either classified or had been carefully cleansed of anything that might hint at involvement. Those who remained were the bit players, people who had seen or heard just a little.

Another major handicap was the brilliant covering-up by the entire American government, quite possibly with the cooperation of other governments, including the disgracefully clever trick of creating an atmosphere in which anyone showing more than a casual interest in UFOs was made to look like a fool. And while this made investigation far more difficult than it should have been, it had the unintended positive effect of revealing the crashes to have been real events. Otherwise, why would the government have gone to such lengths to make them appear imaginary?

The proof is out there, somewhere. If at least two men involved in the packing and transporting of wreckage are known to have taken souvenirs, one can assume that others helped themselves to small pieces of unknown material that might someday acquire great value. Some of the material has probably been thrown away by relatives unaware of its true nature. Some of it, though, probably remains hidden away in attic trunks and little boxes and maybe even between the pages of unread books on a shelf.

There are rumors that one or more of the archeology students who stumbled upon the Plains of San Agustin crash pocketed bits of material and later buried them in a cave. Or that a young man who lived near the Corona site picked up pieces over a period of months or years and hid them in a coffee can he kept in his private little cave.

And then there is all the material, including bodies, recovered by the government. One shudders to think that any of it has been disposed of, and so it must be hidden somewhere. More than one person must know the details: where, by whom, and especially why. . . .

This book is certainly not the end. It is merely the most recent step in the complex, frustrating, fascinating search for witnesses and evidence of one of the most amazing events in world history. The search will continue until the facts have been made public.

Introduction

F OR A FEW HOURS on July 8, 1947, the lid was off and it was possible to take a peek inside the mystery. The lid was then slammed back down so firmly and so authoritatively that nearly everyone soon forgot it had ever been off.

The completely unexpected development came from the Public Information Office at the Roswell Army Air Field in southeastern New Mexico. The press release, distributed by public information officer 1st Lt. Walter Haut on the direct orders of base commander Col. William Blanchard, was a shocker:

> The many rumors regarding the flying disc became a reality yesterday when the Intelligence office of the 509th Bomb Group of the Eighth Air Force, Roswell Army Air Field, was fortunate enough to gain possession of a disc through the cooperation of one of the local ranchers and the sheriff's office of Chaves County.
>
> The flying object landed on a ranch near Roswell sometime last week. Not having phone facilities, the rancher stored the disc until such time as he was able to contact the sheriff's office, who in turn notified Maj. Jesse A. Marcel of the 509th Bomb Group Intelligence Office.
>
> Action was immediately taken and the disc was picked up at the rancher's home. It was inspected at the Roswell Army Air Field and subsequently loaned by Major Marcel to higher headquarters.

The news shot out over the teletype wires to every newspaper and radio station in the country. After two weeks of vague reports of unbelievable sights in the sky, here at last was something tangible. Not that any hard-nosed reporter took the preposterous story at face value, but at least it was more than the usual claim by some housewife that she had seen an aluminum disc fly over her backyard. Questions poured into Army Air Forces information offices from Roswell to Washington, and a lot of men in uniform ran around in circles.

About three hours after the story went out, it was canceled and replaced by another, quite different one: The wonderful "flying disc" was nothing more than the radar reflector from a wandering weather balloon that had somehow been misidentified by the first people to see it. There were sighs of relief in offices in the Pentagon as well as in newsrooms where veteran journalists had been trying to deal with some news that didn't fit the established pattern.

U.S. Eighth Air Force headquarters at Fort Worth, Texas, then became the center of activity. Pieces of the remains of whatever-it-was were flown there from Roswell in a B-29 Superfortress, one of the airplanes operated by the 509th Bomb Group, which was the sole unit in the world equipped to deliver atomic weapons. It had been the B-29s of the 509th that had dropped A-bombs on Hiroshima and Nagasaki.

Major Marcel flew to Fort Worth with the wreckage he had helped recover from the ranch crash site, and it was shown to Eighth Air Force commander Brig. Gen. Roger Ramey. He had a small quantity of it placed in an office and permitted press photographers to take pictures from a distance, while forbidding them to get close enough to touch it. The office was closed briefly, then reopened so that the press could see wreckage close-up and even handle it.

Warrant Officer Irving Newton was called in from his post as base weather officer and promptly identified the wreckage as a radar reflector from a weather balloon known as a rawinsonde. It was used to determine the speed and direction of high-altitude winds and was a standard piece of equipment in those days.

General Ramey went on a Fort Worth radio station to explain

what had happened and to calm things down, though his announced plan to broadcast over the NBC network was never carried through.

While this was going on, wreckage was packed up and loaded into an airplane to be flown to Wright Field in Dayton, Ohio, home of the USAAF's scientific labs. The press reported all of this and unanimously concluded that it had all been a mistake, that a balloon had been misidentified as a flying disc.

According to the July 9 Washington *Post* "[Rancher William] Brazel found the broken remains of the weather device scattered over a square mile of his land. . . . He bundled the tinfoil and broken wooden beams on the kite and the torn synthetic rubber remains of the balloon together and rolled it under some brush. . . ."

As far as the press and the public were concerned, that was the end of the tale of the crashed "flying saucer." No one thought to question why something so commonplace as a weather balloon had caused so much commotion. Or how two officers of an elite AAF unit could possibly have failed to recognize it. Or how this small, flimsy contraption, which could hardly have come to earth violently, could have strewn its pieces over "a square mile" of sheep ranch.

Had these questions been asked, the act of slamming the lid closed might not have been so effective. But they weren't, and the flying saucer wave of 1947 was allowed to die out. For more than two weeks, the papers and news broadcasts had been full of fascinating, fanciful-sounding stories of peculiar flying objects, and nothing had come of it. It was time to move on to other matters. The baseball pennant races were in full swing, and both the press and the public were familiar with them and knew how to handle news of pinch-hit homers and shutouts. Flying discs made everyone just a little uncomfortable.

1

A History of Modern Sightings

B EFORE THERE WERE UFOs, there were remarkable meteors, mystery airships, mystery airplanes, Foo fighters, ghost rockets, flying discs, and flying saucers. In fact, strange, unidentified sights in the sky can be traced as far back into history as one is willing to delve. Drawings interpreted as someone's idea of spaceships and spacemen have been found on the walls of European caves dating back tens of thousands of years. Prehistoric lines on a Peruvian plain are said to be a guide for UFO landings. Biblical passages are read as the appearances of what are now called UFOs. All through the nineteenth century, ships' captains and astronomers reported seeing things in the sky that failed to fit anything known and were thus lamely referred to as "remarkable meteors."

Unfortunately, there is no way to apply scientific techniques to determine the legitimacy of clues older than a few score years. The original references are too vague and the witnesses long since dead, so all that remains are amusing tales and the intriguing hint of a link between ancient unknowns and their modern counterparts. To take old reports at face value would be unscientific in the extreme. The author and philosopher Charles Fort collected several volumes of anecdotes about

1

pre-1930s mysteries, catalogued them, and left them for later generations to unravel.

At the end of the nineteenth century, with ballooning a popular sport and powered balloons—airships—being tested in hopes of providing elementary air transportation, a wave of sightings of "mystery airships" broke out. While many of the reports were eventually blamed on publicity-seekers and unethical journalists, some reports suggested real machines with performance capabilities greater than anything known to have been flying at the time.

But not until man entered the age of mechanical flight with the first voyages by the Wright Brothers in 1903 could reports of odd aerial sights be judged in the light of rapidly advancing technology. It wasn't until 1911–1912 that airplanes began to be seen in any numbers, and then mainly at air shows where there were people ready to pay for the privilege. This was soon followed by the first of the twentieth-century waves of UFOlike sights. Called "mystery airplanes," they are only now beginning to attract serious attention.

Similar waves of mystery airplanes that failed to conform to known activity were reported from both the United States and Europe in the 1930s, but not until the latter stages of World War II did the press and governments began to pay attention to a cohesive phenomenon: the "foo fighters."

These mysterious, often "playful" balls of light and shining spheres were reported by the experienced crews of American warplanes in both the European and Pacific theaters of war in late 1944 and early 1945. They were said to fly along with our planes and even to play tag with them, singly and in small formations. Not once was there any suggestion that a foo fighter had proved aggressive or even mildly unfriendly. That, in the midst of history's most terrible war, suggested two possible explanations: they were something natural (such as St. Elmo's Fire, the eerie atmospheric discharge of built-up static electricity) or they were insidious enemy machines not quite ready for combat. After all, the sky was full of V-1 buzz bombs and V-2 rockets; who could say what other devilish contraptions the Nazis might be readying?

So many reports of foo-fighter sightings were filed with Army Air Forces Intelligence that higher headquarters had little choice but to take them seriously. The Eighth Air Force, based in England and commanded by famed test and racing pilot Jimmy Doolittle, had a study made of the foo fighters. While no copy has yet come to light, it allegedly concluded that some of them might be experimental German or Japanese weapons that had not reached operational status, while others must be misinterpretations of ordinary sights. (After the war, it was reported that captured enemy documents showed that the Germans and Japanese had been aware of the foo fighters but had concluded the mysterious things were probably Allied weapons!)

Based on what little is known about the episode, about all that can be said with any confidence is that the foo fighters were a wartime idiosyncrasy. Once reports of their sighting ceased to be made, it was easy for everyone to forget about them. The war was over and there were more important matters occupying people's minds.

Then, in the summer of 1946, odd sky sights resumed, this time over the Scandinavian countries. They were soon nicknamed "Swedish ghost rockets" since many of them were said to be long and thin, like rockets. Scores of reports were published in newspapers throughout the region, and soon the Swedish Defense Staff established a secret commission to gather and study the reports. Most people in and out of government suspected they were Soviet devices built with the help of captured Nazi scientists and launched from Peenemunde, the legendary German test base located less than a hundred miles across the Baltic from Sweden.

Detailed information was hard to find, and when the Swedish government clamped down on all publicity (one day after former USAAF general Jimmy Doolittle and former Eisenhower aide Gen. David Sarnoff had met with high Swedish officials), it became almost impossible to find out what was happening. Only in the late 1980s, when secrecy was finally relaxed, did it become apparent that the ghost rockets could not possibly have been Soviet missiles and therefore have to be considered proto-UFOs.

In 1946, however, little was known about the nature and origins of the ghost rockets, and so the few who thought seriously about them assumed there was some connection with presumed Soviet rocket or missile experiments, even though the rocket-shaped UFOs usually flew level like airplanes and made little or no noise. Historians agree that no such tests ever took place at Peenemunde, and to have made any would have recklessly endangered secrecy as well as relations with a traditionally neutral neighbor. But logic does not appear to have played a major role in the public's perception of the story.

The ghost rockets, which eventually were seen as far south as Greece, faded away at the end of 1946, just another peculiar interlude. But strange sky sightings did not. They were reported into the spring of 1947, but very quietly, as the fear of ridicule carried more weight than did the need to make news or record potentially important information.

The slowly simmering pot suddenly boiled over on June 24, 1947, with the historic experience of a veteran mountain pilot in Washington State. Pilot and businessman Kenneth Arnold was helping in the hunt for a lost military transport plane in the vicinity of 14,410-foot Mount Rainier when his attention was captured by the brilliant glint from something in the distance. He forgot the search and concentrated on what now appeared as a formation of nine roundish craft, flying in a line and snaking around a series of mountain peaks Arnold knew well from previous flights.

Their speed amazed him, so he used the sweep second hand of the clock on his instrument panel to determine that they had covered the 48 miles between Mount Rainier and Mount Adams in 1 minute, 42 seconds, which works out to 1,700 mph! At the time, the world speed record for airplanes was only 624 mph; it wouldn't approach 1700 mph for another fifteen years. There were a few experimental and research airplanes capable of flying faster than the official record, but they never flew in formation.

Arnold described the flying motion of the objects as resembling that of saucers skipping across the water; this was picked up by the press and quickly distorted into "flying saucers." The experienced pilot's report of a group of objects having unconventional shape, unconventional flying characteristics, and startling speed attracted the immediate attention of the country—including, one can reasonably assume, the U.S. Army Air Forces.

This report was soon joined by hundreds of others of "flying saucers" or "flying discs," traveling singly or in formations, from every state. Many came from highly qualified observers, such as the pilot and co-pilot of a United Airlines DC-4 and several officers at the secret Army Air Forces test base of Muroc Field, California (later renamed Edwards Air Force Base). The high-water mark of this first American wave of UFO sightings came on the July Fourth weekend, when several hundred sightings were recorded in a few days, continuing at a high rate even after the holiday, although most Americans had returned to work.

The saucers were said to have flown at high speeds and at low speeds, at high and at low altitudes. They flew silently and sometimes with soft whirring or buzzing sounds. But one thing no one reported seeing them do was come into contact with the land, either intentionally as if landing, or unintentionally as when crashing.

Newspapers and radio broadcasts were full of stories about the mysterious flying discs, along with a long list of explanations from scientists who should have known better and ordinary people who couldn't be expected to know what they were talking about. They must be airplanes, or balloons, or ice crystals, or hailstones that had somehow become flattened (no one ever explained how) so they would skim across the sky and give the impression of flying. They might be the glowing tailpipes of jets. They were spots before the eyes. They were optical illusions. Or they were simply the figments of wild imagination.

One thing was obvious: They couldn't possibly be what people were describing! There were no round flying machines, or disc-shaped ones. There wasn't anything that could streak along at 1,700 mph within the atmosphere without making noise. All of this added up to either something outlandish or something imaginary.

For several weeks the saucers and the stories about them flew around the country and almost everyone laughed. Especially news commentators and cartoonists, who had a field day with flying saucers and flying soupbowls and other forms of aerial crockery. Then it ended. The saucers stopped flying. Whatever they were, they hadn't really done anything. They hadn't hurt anyone or dented any fenders or squashed anyone's geraniums. It was almost as if they hadn't been here in the first place. And if they hadn't made any detectable impact on American life, perhaps they were no more than a new form of mass hysteria, similar to that which resulted from Orson Welles' 1938 *War of the Worlds* radio program.

Real things make their presence known in more than fanciful tales. They are recognized by experts. They produce changes. But the "flying saucers" hadn't resulted in a single show of concern from any scientist. The government—mainly the U.S. Army Air Forces—said they were not American experimental airplanes or rockets. The press was nearly unanimously flippant in its treatment of the phenomenon. Who can pay attention to a few casual bystanders when the people who should know and who should be concerned haven't shown a hint of interest?

By all indications, the great "flying saucer" scare of 1947 came and went in a few weeks, leaving behind nothing more tangible than memories. Funny memories and puzzling memories, to be sure. But just memories.

The argument against their existence as anything real and solid seemed pretty obvious: If flying saucers were real and were flying over the United States with regularity, then there should be the occasional crash. All known manmade vehicles crash, and in 1947 the flying saucers were assumed to be manmade, if indeed they were anything at all. If they never crash, and every indication was pointing to a complete lack of accidents, then it would seem they couldn't be actual, manmade devices.

If they weren't something manufactured by the U.S., the USSR, or anyone else, they must be some mixture of mis-identified atmospheric and astronomical phenomena: clouds, birds, meteors, stars, planets. The only other possibility was one that no one suggested seriously at the time: that they might be extraterrestrial spacecraft.

2

The Search for Evidence Begins

"T HE PERSON you really ought to talk to is Jesse Marcel. He handled pieces of one of those things."

The remark seemed to come out of nowhere, made in such a matter-of-fact manner that it briefly stumped the gregarious nuclear physicist Stanton Friedman. He had been researching and lecturing about UFOs to hundreds of colleges and professional, educational, and scientific groups for eleven years and thought he was prepared for almost anything, including reports of crashed alien craft. "I didn't know what to make of the statement, so I said, 'Who's he?' "

It was February 20, 1978. Friedman was in Baton Rouge, Louisiana, to present a talk he called "Flying Saucers *Are* Real" at Louisiana State University that evening. He was doing a series of radio and television interviews as part of the advance promotion for the talk and had paused for coffee with the director of one of the TV stations when this remark was made during an otherwise casual conversation.

The station director explained that Marcel had been a major in the Army Air Forces "and handled the wreckage of one of those things," meaning a crashed flying saucer. Marcel was no stranger who had called the station on an impulse and blurted

out this improbable tale. "We're ham radio buddies," the director explained. "I've known him for years; he's a very reliable
person."

Now, a lot of people have flying-saucer stories in readiness
for anyone they have reason to think won't laugh at them,
especially a pro-UFO scientist. Stories of funny lights seen
while driving across the desert at night. Stories of acquain-
tances who claim to know someone who worked with a guy
who said he knows where the bodies of a "flying saucer" crew
are stored. Stories that may be intriguing, but lack substance or
any basis for follow-up. Stories that frustrate far more than
they educate.

This wasn't the first crashed-saucer tale Friedman had heard
in his eleven years of lecturing and listening. As a matter of
fact, there had been several of them, but none had turned out
to lead to any valuable evidence. In 1978 claims of the recovery
of crashed saucers bordered on the disreputable, so Friedman
parked this one in his memory and went on to the university
to deliver his lecture, one of hundreds he gave to college groups
in the 1970s.

"The very next day," Friedman recalled, "while at an airport
on [the way] to my next lecture, I called Information, got a
number for a Jesse Marcel in Houma, Louisiana, and gave him a
call." The lead obviously hadn't slipped very far back in his
mind, and came back to the surface because there was something special about it. "[Marcel] sounded straightforward. He
mentioned that he was the base security officer at Roswell
Army Air Field, in New Mexico, but he couldn't recall the
exact date of the crash ... other than that it was in the late
forties.

"He said he got a phone call from the sheriff's office while he
was eating lunch at the officers' club. The sheriff said that this
rancher had come in with some strange pieces of wreckage and
that there was a lot of it out on his ranch. The sheriff thought
that maybe the base would be interested."

Jesse explained that he went to the office of the Chaves
County sheriff, talked to the rancher, looked at a small piece of

the wreckage, and then talked to his boss back at the air base. He was told to take one of the Counter-Intelligence Corps men and go out and see what this stuff was. Major Marcel did just that, with an officer named Cavitt (he couldn't remember his first name; everybody just called him Cav). They drove out to the ranch, arrived as night was falling, shared a can of beans, slept overnight in their sleeping bags, and the next morning drove with the rancher out to the wreckage site where they found a lot of the material in small pieces.

Marcel described the material to Friedman over the phone, giving the veteran UFO investigator the first indication of the nature of what could possibly turn out to be the most important discovery of the millennium. The area covered with wreckage was roughly three quarters of a mile long and several hundred yards wide. The material Marcel and Cavitt saw was nothing but unusual and thoroughly unrecognizable. Much of it was foil-like: as thin as the foil in a pack of cigarettes, just as light, and yet extremely strong. There were short lengths of I beam with odd symbols along the web. There was other material that somewhat resembled parchment—heavy paper— and, like the foil and the beams, was extremely light and strong. Neither experienced airman had ever seen anything remotely like any of this.

"[Marcel]" Friedman continued, "was checking around for an indication of a crater or [other disturbance in the terrain], "There wasn't one. It seemed to him that it must have exploded in the air. They gathered up a bunch of this stuff in an army Jeep Carry-All and an old Buick staff car and brought it back to town. The next day Marcel was instructed by Col. Blanchard, commanding officer of the air base, to put the stuff in a B-29 and fly it to Wright Field, Ohio (site of the Army Air Forces scientific and technical laboratories, where unfamiliar materials could be studied by experts). A stop was scheduled in Fort Worth, Texas, at the headquarters of the Eighth Air Force, of which they were a part.

"When they got to Texas, Brig. Gen. Roger Ramey, who was head of the Eighth Air Force, told him not to say anything.

Marcel wouldn't, being under orders. And General Ramey told the press it was just a radar reflector from a weather balloon. Just junk. Marcel said, 'I couldn't say anything. It sure wasn't part of a weather balloon; I knew that. But I didn't know what it was. We came back to Roswell. My picture was in the papers all over the place,' he added, 'and I still don't know what it was!' "

Friedman asked Jesse Marcel a few questions and then tucked it all away in that special place reserved for fascinating leads that lack any hope for verification. He had tracked stories of crashed saucers before, like the one about a dozen alien bodies hidden away in the probably-mythical Hangar 18 at Wright-Patterson Air Force Base—the same Wright Field, since renamed, to which the Roswell material reportedly had been flown. All the stories seemed to end the same way, with the main source saying something on the order of "Somebody told me the story, but you can't use his name. No, you can't talk to him. There's no way to verify it, and so you'll just have to take it at face value." That sort of information is worthless until there is something or someone to back it up. One person's testimony simply isn't sufficient to make such a report worth more than scribbled notes.

And so Friedman found it hard to get very excited when he heard Marcel's story, even though it and Marcel sounded straight. There was no date, not even an approximate one, attached to the report. And Friedman was busy tracking down a lot of other seemingly more promising leads.

But this tale, weak as it seemed, kept gnawing away at Friedman. There was something about *crash* and *New Mexico* that added up to more than just three words. Maybe it was because New Mexico, after World War II, was the scene of so much secret work that might be of interest to those of unknown origin and purpose. There was the vast White Sands proving ground, where the U.S. Army was launching captured German V-2 rockets in the first phase of what would become the great American space program. And there was Trinity Site, where the world's first nuclear device was set off, and Los Alamos, where the A-bomb was created in amazing secrecy during the war and where far more powerful weapons were being developed. Friedman had visited Los Alamos while working on the nuclear rocket program a decade earlier and had noted the huge selection of UFO-related materials in the lab's library. Or perhaps it was other places in the state where so much work was being done on advanced types of radar and who-knows-what-else.

Altogether, it added up to the relatively centralized location of the nation's, indeed the world's most advanced technology, all of which was aimed at creating weapons of enormous destructive power and the capacity for interplanetary flight. Certainly all of this would be of great interest to whoever was flying around in disc-shaped craft, be they Russians or aliens. Way back in Stanton Friedman's mind there were a few little clicks, including another lead he had picked up a few years before that might be connected with Marcel's story. It had come about when he was working on a series of magazine articles with West Coast writer Bobbi Slate Gironda. She had heard an interesting UFO anecdote from a Southern California forest ranger named Sleppy. "The person you really ought to talk to is my mother, Lydia Sleppy," he told her.

Together they located Lydia, who told them a story of having been in New Mexico, working at an Albuquerque radio station. One of the people at their Roswell affiliate called up and told her to put a story on the teletype wire about the recovery of a crashed flying saucer that was being sent to Wright Field. He dictated the story and she started to send it out when her transmission was interrupted. Apparently the FBI was monitoring those lines, which was no surprise in view of all the classified work then going on in New Mexico. They told her: "Do not complete this transmission." And she did as she was told, for people in that part of the country were very security-conscious even if they didn't work for the government.

Sometime later, when Mrs. Sleppy talked to the man who had dictated the story to her, he clammed up completely and refused to say anything more about it. This was a puzzling story, to be sure, though not much more so than a lot of other rumors in the flying saucer mill that usually dissolved upon close inspection. Still, this one included the names of some of the people she had worked with, the sort of specific information consistently and conspicuously absent from most other stories.

Friedman tracked down some of the names, which required considerable effort because of the years that had passed since the event, but he soon found himself stonewalled. There was no place to go. One person wouldn't talk at all (intriguingly suspicious, but hardly proof of anything), while another had no additional leads and only vaguely remembered the incident. Was this just another of the many stories that start out sounding so good and end up hanging in midair?

Still, the Jesse Marcel anecdote could turn out to be both true and important. If the major was who he claimed to be, he could have been in a position to know what happened (assuming, of course, that something actually happened). But was he who he claimed to be, or did he have an unfortunately active imagination? And even if he was legitimate, did his story have any connection with that of Lydia Sleppy? Did they even happen in the same year? Could it all be a mistake or garbled information?

Those and many more doubts clouded the issue and kept Friedman from assuming he was finally onto the trail. Until some of the doubts were cleared up, it wouldn't be anything to write home about. Marcel's story certainly sounded exciting and important, but Friedman had no reason to connect it with anything else, because it lacked so much as an approximate date. It was filed away, but with a gold star so it could be retrieved on short notice, should the need arise.

Later that year, on October 24, 1978, Friedman gave a lecture at Bemidji (Minnesota) State University and was approached cautiously by a couple who had left the hall at the end of his talk and then decided to return. They asked, after most of the crowd had departed, if he had ever heard of a saucer that crashed in New Mexico ... with alien bodies. "I've heard rumors about such stories." he responded. "Tell me more." It was one of several stock replies prepared for hints of odd events that frequently came to light in the open atmosphere of a well-attended UFO lecture.

Vern and Jean Maltais told him briefly that a very good friend of theirs, "Barney" Barnett, had related a story of seeing a crashed saucer with alien bodies down in New Mexico in the late forties. They too were unable to pin down a specific year, let alone a month or day. But they stressed that Barnett, an engineer working for the government, was a well-respected individual. They had no reason to think he was telling them anything other than the truth, despite the bizarre content of the story. Crashed saucers are one thing, and could well turn out to be futuristic American or even foreign aircraft or missiles. But alien bodies are another matter entirely, and hardly subject to misinterpretation. Bodies are either people or they are not.

The Maltais had kept in touch with Barnett for several years, though he was dead now. They thought Friedman might be interested in the story, and they were right. Pieces, as yet completely unconnected, were starting to pile up. He took their names and the next day, when he ran into William Moore, a local high school teacher whose interest in UFOs he had known about for years, he suggested that Moore start looking into the Maltais/Barnett story. Friedman and Moore had met a decade earlier, when Friedman was working on nuclear rockets for Westinghouse and involved with a UFO investigation group composed mainly of scientists. He and Moore renewed their acquaintance at a pizza parlor in Minnesota.

In January 1979 Moore happened onto another story that might be connected with the slowly jelling crash report. He began corresponding with Hughie Green, an English flyer and entertainer who had mentioned something odd in his autobiography. While driving across the United States shortly after World War II, Green said, he heard radio reports of the recovery of a crashed saucer somewhere in the American West. Greene was particularly puzzled by his inability to learn more about the story when he arrived on the East Coast. Moore's ques-

tioning brought out the approximate date—early July 1947—
but no more information. Here was another piece of some
puzzle (or possibly of several different puzzles), but so far the
pieces were small, vague, and widely scattered. They formed
nothing approaching a coherent shape. But even these few bits
of data were an improvement on all previous stories of crashed
saucers.

Then, on February 10, 1979, while Moore was rooting
through the newspaper files in the main library of the University of Minnesota, he came across several clippings describing
much the same thing Jesse Marcel had outlined to Stan Friedman a year earlier. It was the breakthrough they had been
looking for.

Jesse Marcel apparently was exactly who he claimed to be,
and as such was an important cog in a machine whose bare
outline was just starting to take form. He had indeed been in
the right place at the right time to become aware of the crash
and the wreckage and the return of the mysterious material to
Roswell Army Air Field. The one-time intelligence officer of
an elite Army Air Forces unit was exactly the sort of firsthand
witness who could propel the story of the crash into the history
books. After more than thirty years the fortress of official
secrecy had developed its first crack.

The clippings opened up all sorts of opportunities for additional investigation. The name of the rancher on whose property the thing had crashed was there: William "Mac" Brazel.
There were several important military people, including
Eighth Air Force commander Brig. Gen. Roger Ramey; his chief
of staff, Col. Thomas Jefferson DuBose; Roswell base commander Col. William Blanchard, and public information officer
1st Lt. Walter Haut—who had issued the puzzling announcement about the recovery of the remains of a "flying disc." If any
of these men could be located and persuaded to talk, the case
could gain a great deal of substance.

What followed was an intensive effort to dig out facts and
supporting information, using the sadly limited resources
available at this stage of the game. First, Friedman and Moore

had to track down people, mostly military, more than thirty years after the fact. Of those who were still living, how many could be found? And if any could be located, would they be willing to talk about a matter almost certainly wrapped tightly in "national security" considerations? As members of the 509th Bomb Group, they had been more security-conscious than almost any others, having been entrusted with many of the secrets of atomic bombs, dropped history's only two nuclear weapons in wartime, and participated in postwar A-bomb tests in the Pacific. They lived with high security twenty-four hours a day.

The obvious first step was to get back to retired Lt. Col. Jesse Marcel, for they knew where he lived and that he was willing to discuss the details he knew of the crash ... unless parties unknown had gotten to him in the interim and convinced him he would be better off keeping quiet. He had details that were assuming great significance as the reality of the event became established. Moore talked with him in the middle of February 1979 and soon got in contact with his son, Jesse, Jr., a medical doctor, pilot, and aircraft-accident investigator. Only eleven at the time of the crash, he nevertheless had knowledge of part of the story, and now, as a leading member of his community, he was highly regarded by all who knew him.

In April 1979 Dr. Marcel wrote to Moore with additional information:

> In reference to our recent phone conversation regarding the UFO incident of 1947 I omitted one startling description of the wreckage for fear that it might have been [interpreted as] the fanciful imagination of an 11-year-old. Imprinted along the edge of some of the beam remnants, there were hieroglyphic-type characters. I recently questioned my father about this, and he recalled seeing these characters also, and even described them as being a pink or purplish-pink color. Egyptian hieroglyphics would be a close visual description of the characters, except that I don't think there were any animal figures present, as there are in true Egyptian hieroglyphics.
>
> I keep wondering if some remnants of the crash might still be

lying on the New Mexico desert floor. According to my father, some of it was left behind when he and his crew visited the crash site. I suspect, however, that after the true nature of the craft became known to Air Force Intelligence, the whole site was gone over with a vacuum cleaner.

As early as 1979 it was becoming evident not only that something very mysterious had been retrieved from the New Mexico desert in 1947, but also that additional information about it was only compounding the mystery instead of elucidating it. The "true nature of the craft" was only being hinted at, with talk of "alien bodies" and now strange symbols on pieces of the wreckage.

But hints were all that were known. Two men had testified to their personal contact with the peculiar wreckage; two men with good reputations and good reasons to have been in position to have seen pieces of the wreckage. But just two men. Hardly enough to constitute an airtight case that could be taken into court. Still, people were beginning to talk after thirty years, and the prospects for further disclosures were looking up.

The key, of course, was the senior Marcel, the value of whose revelations rested upon his personal stature and reliability. Far from being the sort to blurt out classified information, he had been a trusted career military man who had been promoted from major to lieutenant colonel shortly after the crash episode. He was then assigned to a vital, high-level program that collected data in a search for evidence that the Soviet Union had exploded its first nuclear weapon. "When we finally detected [that] there had been a nuclear explosion," he told reporter Bob Pratt in 1979, "I had to write a report on it. In fact, I wrote the very report that President Truman read on the air declaring Russia had exploded an atomic device." This report shattered the complacency of the nation, as most scientists and government officials assumed the United States would have several more years of its monopoly on weapons of mass destruction.

Once Jesse Marcel Sr. had spoken out on the crash and his involvement in it, his son was under no pressure to keep this novel family secret, even though he was now part of the military as a National Guard helicopter pilot and Vietnam veteran. Neither man has indicated that any pressure was applied to keep them from talking further, nor that Jesse Sr. ever felt that national security was being endangered by his speaking out.

The first stage of the investigation of the crash at Corona had ended. Not that a great number of details had been disclosed, but the reality of the crash of something very strange had been established with sufficient authority to elevate this case to a height never approached by any other story of the crash of a flying saucer. It could yet turn out to be a mistake, the crash of a test rocket carrying a monkey, which had been exaggerated through sloppy retelling—but the chances of that being the case were diminishing. In the past, careful investigation had always revealed major flaws in a crash report. This time, each new piece of information tended to support the premise that this might well be the big one.

So far, however, there wasn't enough information considered sufficiently reliable to justify going public. All that was known with any degree of certainty was that something odd had crashed in New Mexico in early July 1947; that according to an official press release, it had been recovered by the Army Air Forces; and that it had been flown away, probably to Wright Field near Dayton, Ohio. It was also known that official denials followed quickly and had been accepted. Friedman, having worked under serious secrecy rules for fourteen years, knew the government could keep secrets under some pretty emotional conditions. But a crashed flying saucer and alien bodies?

The questions triggered by even this small amount of information were now bubbling to the surface:

1. Would the Marcels stick to their story? Or would they recant, or claim to have been misquoted when the time came to stand up and be counted?
2. Could enough confirming witnesses be found to sub-

stantiate the Marcels' story in a way that would be widely accepted?

3. Was the recovered material really as unusual as suggested, or could it be explained as something generally unknown at the time but subsequently accepted as commonplace?

4. Would the U.S. government, once the story began to emerge into the public eye, be able to explain the "crash" as some normal event in such convincing terms that all thoughts of alien spacecraft would be put to rest?

5. Exactly what was found at the Brazel ranch?

6. Where was the material taken, and what was done with it (and to it) prior to its being shipped from the Southwest?

7. Who was involved in the analysis of the material, and how were they selected?

8. What was done with the material when the scientific work on it was completed?

9. Were bodies found? If so, what were they like and what was done with them?

10. Who was responsible for the grand cover-up of the crash and its aftermath? And what was the claimed justification for keeping all news of the crash and its investigation completely secret from the American people for more than forty years?

11. What was it doing in New Mexico in the first place?

12. Was it one of the many "flying saucers" seen all around the United States during late June and early July 1947?

3

The Government and UFOs

THE MULTITUDE of vital questions surrounding the crashes in New Mexico is a recent phenomenon; at the time, almost no attention was paid the events.

News reports about the recovery of one crashed disc, then the official announcement that it was nothing more exciting than the radar reflector from a weather balloon, were accepted as part of the dizzy, confusing swirl of flying-saucer stories. None of these reports, from the very first by Kenneth Arnold on June 24 through the end of the 1947 sighting wave a few weeks later, made a bit of sense to the great majority of Americans. They lacked the technical sophistication of their children and grandchildren, and also their descendants' broad suspicion of the government. As a result, they were unable to see the reports as more than harmless foolishness.

High-performance airplanes—jets, in particular—were just beginning to proliferate, and as yet were seen mainly near military airfields and at air shows. The day of the huge jet airliner packed with casually dressed vacationers was not merely far in the future but also considered only in magazine articles about the wonders of science to come. As for spaceships from other planets? They were the stuff of comic books, no more.

Few people thought the flying discs might be anything truly new and different. Rather, they were seen as a mixture of mistakes and sensationalism. And if strange craft of unknown origins and purposes were *not* flying over America, why pay any attention to a quickly denied claim that one had crashed? Something that doesn't exist can't very well crash, can it? It would be almost half an average lifetime before more than a few people began to think much about UFOs being fallible.

Publicly, it looked like the flying saucers had flown back to nowhere at the end of the 1947 wave of sightings. No one in a position of authority—government officials, scientists, respected newsmen—had suggested that there might be anything more to them than a brief, particularly frivolous fad. It had been a lot of fun and now it was over . . . except for those who had seen things they could not explain. Ted Bloecher's landmark study of the newspaper coverage of the 1947 flying saucer furor showed that almost a thousand reports of strange sights had been made to someone. In addition, there may have been several times that many people who had seen odd flying things but not mentioned them out of fear of ridicule. But that still totals no more than a few thousand people who had their own personal reasons for believing that the flying saucers were anything more than imagination fueled by excitement.

Completely unknown to the American people was the very serious interest being shown in the flying saucers by the U.S. Army Air Forces. Officially, the government continued to scoff at flying-saucer reports and their reporters, and it would be many years before any of this became public knowledge, for the whole matter was treated as a vital military secret. Even before the June–July 1947 sighting wave had run its course, the first of several official inquiries had been started. Its conclusion, had it been presented to the general public, would have created shock waves: "From detailed study of reports selected for their impression of veracity and reliability, several conclusions have been formed: This 'flying saucer' situation is not at all imaginary or seeing too much in some natural phenomena. *Something is really flying around."* (Emphasis added)

This statement was in an official document dated July 30, 1947, and was based on a study of just fifteen sightings of flying saucers (mainly from pilots) between May 19 (five weeks *before* Kenneth Arnold's highly publicized report that kicked off the modern UFO era) and July 10. It produced considerable information on the appearance and behavior of things that 99.99 percent of the people had been convinced were imaginary:

1. The appearance of these objects is metallic, indicating a metallic skin, at least.
2. When a trail is observed, it is lightly colored, a blue-brown haze, that is similar to a rocket engine's exhaust. Contrary to a rocket of the solid type, one observation indicates that the fuel may be throttled, which would indicate a liquid rocket engine.
3. As to shape, all observations state that the object is circular or at least elliptical, flat on the bottom and slightly domed on the top. The size estimates place it somewhere near the size of a C–54 or Constellation [1940s airliners having a wingspan of 120 feet and length of 95 feet].
4. Some reports describe two tabs, located at the rear and symmetrical about the axis of flight motion.
5. Flights have been reported, with three to nine of them, flying good formation on each other, with speeds always above 300 knots (350 mph).
6. The discs oscillate laterally when flying along, which could be snaking.

The U.S. Army Air Forces, fresh from a major share of the victory in history's largest and most violent air war, was baffled by some high-performance craft flying through skies it rightfully considered its own. The flying saucers or flying discs or flying whatevers were fast and maneuverable and thus capable of evading American interceptors with ease. It requires little imagination to picture the consternation that must have swept through the offices of high-ranking Army Air Forces people in

Washington when faced with this mysterious incursion that had to be considered a potential threat.

What could they say when President Harry Truman asked them what in hell was going on? They couldn't claim to know what the flying saucers were, for they would then have to provide details they didn't have. They also couldn't very well admit that there were unknown craft flying through American skies with impunity, for the ensuing questions would be far too embarrassing to contemplate. What if the Senate Armed Services and Appropriations committees got wind of the USAAF's inability to cope with foreign machines flying over American cities? The Army Air Force was about to achieve a long-term dream and become a separate service: the United States Air Force. An admission of such impotence could wipe that out overnight and leave the once-proud flyboys huddled in a few offices in the basement of the Department of Agriculture.

The only solution was to launch an all-out effort to find out what the flying saucers were, and to keep the entire matter totally secret from the public and from most of the government until the USAAF could regain control of the skies.

Less than two months later, on September 23, 1947, a more detailed report was prepared by the Air Force's Air Materiel Command (the technical and scientific establishment) for Air Force Intelligence. It reiterated the conclusions of the first report and would also have amazed the public if it had not been kept secret: "The phenomenon is something real and not visionary or fictitious."

While the American people and most of their leaders remained in total ignorance of the extent of official concern and activity, yet another step was taken to expand the knowledge of peculiar flying things which hardly anyone outside the Pentagon considered of any consequence. On October 28, 1947, a draft order was prepared for American intelligence operatives throughout the world, directing them to get all potentially relevant information about flying saucers. The order was an intelligence collection memorandum from Brig. Gen. George Schulgen, chief of the USAF's Air Intelligence Requirements

Division and was based on a summary of flying-saucer characteristics supplied him by Lt. Gen. Nathan Twining, commander of the Air Materiel Command.

Within the order was the first known official mention of the possibility that some of the flying saucers might be extraterrestrial spacecraft:

> This strange object, or phenomenon, may be considered, in view of certain observations, as long-range aircraft capable of a high rate of climb, high cruising speed and highly maneuverable and capable of being flown in very tight formations. For the purpose of analysis and evaluation of these so-called "flying saucers," the object sighted is being assumed to be a manned craft of unknown origin. While there remains the *possibility* of Russian manufacture, based on perspective thinking and actual accomplishments of the Germans, *it is the considered opinion of some elements that the object may in fact represent an interplanetary craft of some kind.* [Emphasis added]

Moreover, within the order are several references that make little sense unless read in the context of presumed knowledge of a flying saucer that crashed several months earlier in New Mexico. These are shown in boldface in the following partial breakdown of the types of information being sought by USAF Intelligence:

Construction.
a. Type of material, whether metal, ferrous, non-ferrous or non-metallic.
b. Composite or sandwich construction utilizing various combinations of metals, **metallic foils,** plastics, and perhaps **balsa wood or similar material.**
c. Unusual fabrication methods to achieve **extreme light weight and structural stability.**

Arrangement.
a. Special provisions such as **retractable domes** to provide unusual observation for the pilot and crew members.

b. **Unusual features or provisions regarding the opening and closing of doors.**

Landing Gear.
a. Indicate type of landing gear—whether conventional, tricycle, multiple wheel, etc., or of an unconventional type such as **tripod** or skid.
b. Provisions for takeoff from ice, snow, sand or water.

Powerplant.
a. (3. Nuclear propulsion (atomic energy). Atomic energy engines would probably be unlike any familiar type of engine, although atomic energy might be employed in combination with any of the above types (piston, jet). Aircraft **would be characterized by lack of fuel systems and fuel storage space.**
b. The powerplant **would likely be an integral part of the aircraft and possibly not distinguishable as an item separate from the aircraft.**

Visual observations of the exterior of a flying craft—especially brief ones made at long range—could not possibly have suggested that flying saucers have *extreme light weight and structural stability,* or *have doors that operate in an unusual fashion,* nor be built from *metallic foils or balsa wood or similar materials.* And as for suspecting that an atomic energy engine "would likely be an integral part of the aircraft," this would take close-up inspection in order to get even a hint that such might be the case. A pilot or ground observer, no matter how skilled and experienced, simply cannot detect this sort of thing when a flying machine shoots past.

Unfortunately, clues that are kept secret do not lead anywhere. It would be almost two generations before any of this began to point toward the truth.

Had this intelligence collection memorandum been common knowledge in 1947, it could have changed the course of history by establishing the reality of the New Mexico crash. But it was kept secret until 1985, so there was no opportunity for anyone outside some double-locked doors in the Pentagon to ponder the clues and their possible meaning. Or to wonder why Air Force Intelligence was asking its agents to look for things that were not even hinted at in any known study of flying saucers, nor described in any sighting reports made prior to creation of the memorandum.

The gap between what was happening and what was known on the outside grew wider and wider. Two weeks after Kentucky National Guard pilot Capt. Thomas Mantell died in the crash of his P-51 Mustang while trying to check out a UFO reported by hundreds of people, the first known long-term investigation of UFOs was established on January 22, 1948 at Wright Field. Because it was classified, Project Sign was known publicly as Project Saucer, the purpose of which was said to be to collect reports from persons inside and outside the government and attempt to tie them to conventional sights: airplanes, balloons, clouds, planets, meteors, optical illusions, hoaxes, and so on.

Sometime around August 1948 staff members of Project Sign produced their eventually legendary Top Secret Estimate of the Situation, which allegedly concluded that the saucers were probably extraterrestrial. It went all the way up to the Chief of Staff, Gen. Hoyt Vandenberg, who rejected its conclusion as lacking evidence. All copies were ordered destroyed, though rumors persist that at least one may have survived.

On October 7, 1948, after Project Sign had been in operation for almost nine months, a letter was sent by Col. H. H. McCoy, intelligence chief of the Air Materiel Command (which included Project Sign) to the Central Intelligence Agency. Classified Secret, it contained an admission in direct contrast to almost everything the U.S. government has ever said on the subject:

"This Headquarters is currently engaged in an intelligence investigation of all reported unidentified aerial phenomena. *No concrete evidence as to the exact identity of any of the reported objects has been received. Similarly, the origin of the so-called 'flying discs' remains obscure.*" (Emphasis added)

Two months later, on December 10, 1948, the USAF's Directorate of Intelligence issued a lengthy Analysis of Flying Object Incidents in the U.S. that remained Top Secret until 1985. It made no attempt to explain individual reports but strongly suggested that hypothetical Soviet developments based on captured Nazi German technology were responsible for flying saucer sightings. Singled out for particular attention were the experimental craft (mainly gliders) developed by the Horten brothers, despite the fact that they were characterized by very long, thin wooden wings and resembled almost no reported saucers.

The view in some circles is that the report may be similar to the earlier Top Secret Estimate of the Situation that had been rejected, with the material about the extraterrestrial nature of the saucers replaced by that about Soviet/Nazi craft which would have been more palatable to the Air Force brass.

All was assumed to be proper in the operation of Project Sign and its successor, Project Grudge, until late December 1949, when noted aviation writer and retired Marine Corps pilot Donald Keyhoe made a series of startling accusations in *True* magazine. He cited inside sources who led him to the conclusion that the flying saucers were alien spacecraft bent on exploring Earth. A similar claim had been made earlier in an obscure occult magazine, but the *True* piece was read by hundreds of thousands and was then picked up by the wire services and made into front-page news.

Neither before nor since has the U.S. government reacted so swiftly and definitively to a popular-magazine article challenging its handling of the UFO problem. To counter Keyhoe's claims, the Department of Defense quickly announced:

The Air Force has discontinued its special project investigating and evaluating reported "flying saucers" on the basis that there is no evidence the reports are not the result of natural phenomena. Discontinuance of the project, which was carried out by the Air Force, was concurred in the Departments of the Army and Navy. (In fact, the official investigation was *not* discontinued but merely deemphasized.)

The Air Force said that all evidence and analyses indicate that the reports of unidentified flying objects are the result of:

(1) Misinterpretation of various conventional objects.
(2) A mild form of mass hysteria.
(3) Or hoaxes.

The Air Force said that continuance of the project is unwarranted since additional incidents now are simply confirming findings already reached.

Available with the press release was the 600-page Project Grudge report, which included information on 237 UFO cases—55 of which remained unexplained. Moreover, many of the explanations for reports were scientifically weak, if not faulty.

The first doubts about the sincerity of the government's efforts to understand flying saucers had arisen. But since almost none of the original case files were available for independent evaluation, little could be done to support the slowly growing suspicions. Any developments within the official investigation were effectively concealed as the reports continued to stream into the office at Wright-Patterson Air Force Base. They were categorized as "explained", "insufficient information," or "unknown", then quietly filed away for purposes yet to be understood. The evidence strongly suggests that Projects Sign, Grudge, and Blue Book almost certainly constituted a public relations front intended to pacify a concerned public rather than a scientific study to determine if UFOs were a threat to the national security, as its proponents insisted in countless news releases and press conferences.

In 1952 the name of the investigation was changed from Grudge to Blue Book, and as such it would achieve fame and infamy far beyond what the government could have intended or expected. Its conscientious new director, Capt. Edward Ruppelt, would be at the center of more controversy than the Air Force was prepared to handle. It began with an upswing in sighting reports in early 1952 and built as activity surged to unprecedented levels in July and August.

With fifteen hundred reports to Project Blue Book for all of 1952 and as many as forty per day at the height of the wave, the limited facilities of the little office were swamped. Cases were stacked up after having been scanned and "explained" with little regard for the facts. Huge, violently maneuvering spheres were called "balloons," while discs that hovered silently and then streaked away were called "possible aircraft." The situation was out of control even before UFOs appeared over Washington, D.C., in mid-July, tracked on radar simultaneously from three separate locations as they flitted at will over the White House, the Capitol, and even the Pentagon.

Under heavy pressure to explain what was going on, the U.S. Air Force on July 29 held its largest press conference since World War II. Maj. Gen. John Samford of USAF Intelligence admitted that the UFO sightings were not all imagination: "There have remained a percentage of [the] total, in the order of twenty percent of the reports, that have come from credible observers of relatively incredible things." And who were these "credible observers"? SAMFORD: "I think there might be something like eight percent that come from civil airlines pilots. You might find another percentage, in the order of twenty-five, might come from military pilots." In other words, one of every three persons reporting "relatively incredible things" was a professional pilot, whose eyesight and judgment were regularly checked to make certain he could safely carry out his vital duties.

Here was the first truly public admission from the Air Force that UFO sightings should be taken seriously. But it was overshadowed by the more immediate concern of the gathering of reporters, which was the sightings over Washington. These, Samford implied, were caused by temperature inversions (the source of mirages) that supposedly made lights on the ground appear to be high in the sky. This explanation was widely accepted and served its purpose—to calm the fears of the American people, who were understandably worried about

mysterious things flying over some of the most sensitive buildings in the country.

There was absolutely no science to back up General Samford's theory, but this was known only to a few scientists who
had looked into the matter . . . and they kept quiet. Many years
later, an official Air Force scientific report demolished the
"temperature inversion" explanation for UFOs, but it was not
publicized and thus had no impact.

On the same day the Air Force held its big press conference
the Central Intelligence Agency began a series of hush-hush
meetings to deal with its concern that a flood of UFO reports
could clog the nation's communications channels and be used
by some enemy as a smoke screen to conceal an attack. This
led to the January 1953 meeting of a select group of scientists
under chairman H. P. Robertson that spent several hours studying UFO case files provided by the Air Force. It then announced
(in great secrecy, of course) that they showed no evidence of
being a threat to national security or of being extraterrestrial
spacecraft. The CIA recommended the situation be defused by
removing much of the mystery.

Instead, Project Blue Book adopted an even more restrictive
policy on public information and soon reduced its contact with
the press and the American people to an annual report listing
the percentages of sightings explained as balloons, satellites,
and the like while stressing the lack of evidence that UFOs
were anything more than mistakes. But while the statistics
supported the Air Force's claims of increasing effectiveness,
more and more case files were becoming public knowledge and
illustrating the serious ineptitude of Project Blue Book.

On July 31, 1952, just two days after the Air Force press
conference that paraded the supposed efficiency of Project Blue
Book in explaining UFOs, a memorandum was prepared on the
subject by Brig. Gen. Alfred R. Maxwell of the Research and
Development Board. Until recently it was classified Security
Information Confidential. While it generally supported the
official position that UFO reports contain no information of
value, one statement stands out in stark contrast to the rest of

the memo and to all contemporary and subsequent official statements: ". . . the Air Force has made very little progress in learning what the phenomena or objects are and what causes them." After five years of trying! Had this not remained secret for almost a third of a century after it was written, the stature of the government's overt UFO investigation might not have seemed quite so impressive.

In 1955 the Air Force issued a thick document called Blue Book Special Report 14, a statistical analysis of all the reports received for its first six years. Prepared by the private and respected Battelle Memorial Institute in Columbus, Ohio, and reportedly funded by the Central Intelligence Agency, it was a civilian study of the official data.

Of 2,199 cases considered through the end of 1952, the Air Force's own people had determined that 290 of them (13 percent) could not be explained. The independent Battelle scientists, however, classified 434 (20 percent) as unexplained, and that was boosted to 22 percent when the cases lacking sufficient detail for analysis were eliminated. Either way, a lot of UFO reports remained without satisfactory explanation, despite implications to the contrary in the press release that accompanied the report when it was revealed to the public in October 1955.

"No evidence of the existence of the popularly-termed 'flying saucers' was found." The press release stressed the allegedly improved methods and procedures of early 1955 (a time period having absolutely no connection with Special Report 14). Air Force Secretary Donald Quarles was quoted: "I feel certain that even the unknown three percent [for 1955, not 1947–1952]) could have been explained as conventional phenomena or illusions if more complete observational data had been available." This was in direct contradiction of the way sightings had always been classified, "insufficient data" cases being in their own category and completely separate from the "unknowns."

Perhaps the most telling revelation of the Battelle independent analysis can be found in a set of pie charts illustrating the relationship between the technical qualifications and reliability of the witnesses, and the percentage of unexplained cases. For witnesses rated Poor-to-Doubtful, only 14 percent of the reports couldn't be explained by the Battelle scientists. But for witnesses rated Good-to-Excellent, twice as many—27 percent—couldn't be explained. Clearly, the better the witness, the harder it was to explain a UFO report. Had this instead of irrelevant material been emphasized in the press release, the public might have realized that many UFO reports were still a major mystery to the U.S. Air Force.

Now, if there was a report numbered 14, shouldn't there, by all the laws of logic, be thirteen previous reports? Hints of earlier Project Blue Book reports had been floating around for several years, but so little was known about them that it had to be assumed that if they existed at all, they must still be classified. As there was no way to obtain material classified Confidential, Secret, Top Secret, and so on, a lot of possibly important information was being held back.

Unbeknown to anyone, Project Grudge and Blue Book Reports 1 through 12, dated 1951–1953, had been declassified from Confidential and Secret as early as 1960. But the facts of their writing, classification, and eventual declassification had not been announced. Once the situation became known to National Investigations Committee on Aerial Phenomena (NICAP), an effort was begun through the Government Operations Committee of the House of Representatives to override the refusal of the Air Force to release this unclassified material. Thanks to the assistance of Congress, they were pried loose from the Air Force and published by NICAP in 1968. Report 13 is still the subject of rumors and denials.

Now, for the very first time, there was *proof* that the U.S. government had withheld *unclassified* UFO information from the public. These periodic status reports of Projects Grudge and Blue Book revealed a great deal about the inner workings of the only known official investigation. Moreover, they added considerable weight to a 1958 commercially published book about Project Blue Book by Edward Ruppelt, project director when most of the reports were written. Conflicts within the government on UFO policy were aired, as were some of the failures of the system. Dozens of previously unheard-of UFO reports were opened to debate.

The efficiency and effectiveness of Project Blue Book were brought into question by the project's own words. Those who had long been challenging the Air Force's handling of its UFO investigation suddenly had a storehouse of ammunition provided by the Air Force itself. Public and press confidence in the ability of the government to cope with UFOs dropped to a new low.

In the spring of 1964 another startling news report came out of New Mexico that must have raised considerable consternation at the Pentagon. Patrolman Lonnie Zamora, of the Socorro Police Department, radioed his headquarters that he had seen a landed UFO accompanied by two small, white-suited individuals, parked in a barren area outside town. He said he got close enough to see an "insignia" on the side of the metallic, egg-shaped object before it began to roar and spout flame. Fearing it was about to explode, he ducked down behind his cruiser, then looked up when the noise ceased and saw the craft hovering a few feet in the air and making absolutely no sound.

After it flew away, he walked down to the landing site with a police sergeant who had responded to his radioed call for assistance, and they found burned shrubs, scorched ground, and indentations in the soil corresponding to the location of the object's landing gear.

Within two hours an Army Intelligence agent from the White Sands Proving Ground was there, as was an FBI agent, and their intensive investigation resulted in a lengthy report detailing the event. They were clearly impressed by Officer Zamora, as was Project Blue Book scientific consultant Dr. J. Allen Hynek, who arrived a day later.

Half-hearted official efforts to explain the UFO as a rancher's helicopter or a NASA moon-landing test vehicle were quickly dropped, as neither could possibly account for the main characteristics of the sighting, especially the silent hovering. When

Project Blue Book closed its doors in 1969, this case was still listed as unknown, and the final chief of the project, Maj. Hector Quintanilla, called it the most puzzling report of more than twelve thousand in the files.

The Socorro landing is widely regarded as one of the most impressive and baffling cases of all. As such, it placed such previously "far-out" aspects of the subject as nuts-and-bolts high-performance craft and small humanoid crew members somewhere near the center. This UFO gave every indication of being a solid object . . . something manufactured . . . a machine. There was no need to invoke such esoteric explanations as parallel universes or psychic projections to account for something that looked and acted like a very advanced form of transportation. So advanced that it cannot be understood. But not necessarily so advanced that it might never crash.

In 1965 an effort was begun to rebuild public confidence in the official investigation, which had been badly damaged by repeated disclosures of the failure of Project Blue Book explanations to match the facts on which they were supposed to be based. The upshot was a $500,000-plus government contract to the University of Colorado to study the Air Force investigation—in public. The initially enthusiastic support from the major private UFO groups soon turned sour, as it became apparent that outspoken study director Dr. Edward Condon had concluded well in advance that there was nothing to be learned from investigating UFOs.

When his unscientific attitude could no longer be ignored, two scientist members of the Colorado group went public with a damaging document and were promptly fired. Despite the open controversy, the final report of the Condon Committee was completed in 1968, blessed by the National Academy of Sciences, and then published commercially. Dr. Condon's thoroughly negative summation was in stark contrast to the fascinating data buried in the lengthy report, where 30 percent of the cases were left without conventional explanation. Of more than 550 unexplained reports then in the Project Blue Book files, only three were considered by the University of Colorado, while current sightings having little chance of being significant were given expensive on-the-spot investigations. It was a highly unsatisfying exercise.

While the Condon report was widely accepted as the final word on UFOs, not everyone agreed. The prestigious American Institute of Aeronautics and Astronautics, professional society of the aerospace industry, stated: "The opposite conclusion could have been drawn from its content, namely that a phenomenon with such a high rate of unexplained cases (about 30%) should arouse sufficient scientific curiosity to continue its study."

But the Condon report did its job, which was to give the Air Force an excuse to retire from the increasingly embarrassing UFO-investigating business. On December 17, 1969, Project Blue Book was shut down after almost twenty-two years of collecting reports and combating charges. The final tally showed 12,783 reports received and 585 declared "Unknown." At least several hundred of the so-called explained reports were anything but explained in scientific terms. But once Project Blue Book was disbanded, its files were removed from Wright-Patterson, first to the Air Force Archives at Maxwell AFB, Alabama, and then to the National Archives in Washington, D.C., where all names of witnesses were removed. The open, public involvement of the U.S. Air Force, and indeed the U.S. government, with UFOs was at an end.

The incessant claims by the Air Force that it was no longer concerned with UFOs after 1969 are hollow. A careful reading of the memo that recommended the closing of the project, as well as a staff summary which accompanied it, reveals the true state of affairs.

Brig. Gen. Carroll H. Bolender, Air Force Deputy Chief of Staff for Research and Development, stated on October 20, 1969, that the Air Force investigation (not specifically limited to Project Blue Book) had two objectives: "to determine whether UFOs pose any threat to the security of the United States; and to determine whether UFOs exhibit any unique scientific information or advanced technology which could contribute to scientific or technical research."

He then said that "the continuation of Project Blue Book

cannot be justified, either on the grounds of national security or in the interest of science." He *does not* say that there is no justification for the continuation of other Air Force UFO activity. In fact, he leaves that door wide open: "However, as already stated, reports of UFOs which could affect national security would continue to be handled through the standard Air Force procedures designed for this purpose."

Bolender adds: "The Air Force experience therefore confirms the impression of the University of Colorado researchers that the defense function could be performed within the framework established for intelligence and surveillance operations without the continuation of a special unit such as Project Blue Book."

Clearly, all that happened in December 1969 was that Project Blue Book was ended, while the remainder of Air Force (and other governmental) UFO-related activities no doubt continued unabated, since "reports of unidentified flying objects which could affect national security are made in accordance with JANAP 146 or Air Force Manual 55-11, *and are not part of the Blue Book system*" (emphasis added).

If the national security-related UFO reports never were seen by the people in Project Blue Book, then their contention that UFOs showed no evidence of a threat to national security is empty. And since there was a special procedure for handling UFO reports having national security aspects, then is it possible that UFOs involve some kind of threat to the nation? At the very least, someone must have thought so.

When Project Blue Book shut its doors, it signaled the end of an era. The press and the public, aware only of the totally negative conclusions of the Condon Report and the apparent end of all official interest in UFOs, assumed the subject was dead. There were scattered lingering doubts, especially among those who remained convinced they had seen unexplained things flying through the sky. But for most people, UFOs were about to fade into history.

The major private organization—NICAP—rapidly lost its mass appeal, its funding which came almost entirely from membership fees, and its ability to pressure the government. Its once busy downtown Washington office was closed to permit construction of a station of the new Metro subway system, and its shrinking operations were relocated in a suburb, out of sight.

For several years so little was heard about UFOs that it was as if they had never existed in the first place. Many once-confident UFO activists could hardly be blamed for wondering if they really had been as gullible as the Air Force had so often implied. All but the largest of the civilian groups vanished, and the others shrank into impotence. Sources of information rapidly dried up. If UFOs were still being seen, it was all but impossible to find out anything about them. Maybe they had finally lost interest in human affairs and gone home.

When the Air Force closed Project Blue Book, its position on the controversial matter was the same as it had been for many years, and would remain for many more:

(1) no unidentified flying object reported, investigated and evaluated by the Air Force has ever given any indication of threat to our national security;

(2) there has been no evidence submitted to or discovered by the Air Force that sightings categorized as UNIDENTIFIED represent technological developments or principles beyond the range of present-day scientific knowledge; and

(3) there has been no evidence indicating that sightings categorized as UNIDENTIFIED are extraterrestrial vehicles.

The final word? Not quite! The loopholes are enormous:

1. No threat to national security? Certainly not from cases in the Project Blue Book files. But as for other cases, they would be buried deep in secure filing cabinets and computer databases and could not be referred to in unclassified documents. The mere existence of procedures to deal with reports having national security implications raises a lot of questions the government refuses to address.

2. So what if none of Blue Book's UNIDENTIFIED cases is said to represent evidence of advanced technology? It all depends on its never-specified definition of "technological developments or principles beyond the range of present-day scientific knowledge." No claim is made that sightings categorized as other than UNIDENTIFIED represent advanced technology, and it is certainly possible that one or more classified investigations use other terms to describe such reports.

One is left wondering exactly what it would take to convince the Air Force that within the 585 UNIDENTIFIED reports there *is* evidence beyond present-day knowledge? Do they think disc-shaped, cylindrical and spherical aircraft are within present-day knowledge? That silent supersonic flight can be achieved using what is known about aerodynamics? That long-term hovering followed by astounding acceleration is fully understood by aeronautical engineers? On the contrary, these achievements are far beyond the state of the art, and the big aerospace firms would kill to know how to build aircraft capable of such flight!

3. As for no sightings representing extraterrestrial vehicles ... perhaps this can be supported. But how about *crashes*? Maybe you can't see into a UFO as it flies by to check out the physical characteristics of its crew. But when you find one on the ground, it's another matter. Such cute fiddling with the language may conceal matters of cosmic importance.

There is no evidence that anyone connected with Project Blue Book or its predecessors bothered to study the "unidentified" cases as a group, to see if they amounted to more than a hodgepodge of unrelated anecdotes. Had anyone bothered to make such a study, he certainly would have found distinct patterns of both appearance and behavior displayed by the almost-600 UNIDENTIFIED cases, as well as hundreds more that should have been called "unidentified." This, in turn, would have led straight to the conclusion that the men who looked at the very first "flying disc" reports in the summer of 1947 were correct when they concluded that "something is really flying around."

This, of course would have produced a major embarrassment, for it would have negated decades of pronouncements by official spokespersons who obviously were under strict orders to play down UFOs by any means available. The men at Project Blue Book, and their superiors, were not stupid; they were simply following their orders and being careful not to rock the boat.

It is entirely possible that they were being taken advantage of just as much as the American people who swallowed their lies. After all, it doesn't take a genius to see that the material in the Project Blue Book files can more easily be used to demonstrate that UFOs are highly puzzling than that they have all been explained. It just takes a visit to the microfilm reading room of the National Archives on the Mall in Washington, D.C. The information is there to see and to copy and to analyze.

Clearly, someone in a position of power saw Project Blue Book as a tool for influencing public opinion, rather than as a device for learning about UFOs. When it comes to hiding the truth from the public over a long period of time, it may have no rivals in recorded history. As long as the existence of UFOs can be held up to serious doubt, there is little danger that anyone will take reports of their crashing seriously.

It wasn't just the U.S. government that recognized the crash(es) in New Mexico as an important event. In August 1991 it was revealed in *Rabochaya Tribuna* (*The Workers' Tribune*) published in Moscow, that no less a figure than Soviet dictator Joseph Stalin took the news to heart back in 1947.

The nearly full-page interview with Professor Valery Burdakov, of the Scientific Geoinformation Center of the USSR Academy of Sciences, revealed that Stalin had called in several of his top scientists after the "sensational news generated by the capture of a 'saucer' that purportedly had crashed near Roswell."

These scientists included Sergey Korolyev, designer of the first Soviet military rocket in 1947 and of the launchers that put Sputnik I into space in 1957 and Yuri Gagarin up in 1962. It was he who told Professor Burdakov about Stalin's great interest. Other involved scientists reportedly included M. Tikhonravov, who had been experimenting with liquid-fuel rockets since the early 1930s; Mstislav Keldysh, who worked for Korolyev in 1947 and later became president of the USSR Academy of Sciences; and nuclear physicist Alexandr Topchiyev, who became vice president of the academy.

According to Burdakov, Stalin had several women assigned to Korolyev as translators to help him with "a pile of foreign materials and books" related to the UFO phenomenon, and Burdakov was told that the research had to be done in secrecy. "Several days later, he was invited to come and see Stalin himself," Burdakov said. "Stalin asked him for his opinion and Sergey [Korolyev] replied that, in his view, the UFO is not a weapon of a potential enemy and does not represent any serious danger for the country, but evidently the phenomenon is real."

Korolyev advised Stalin that, when the opportunity arose, the phenomenon should be studied further, and Stalin replied that Korolyev's opinion was similar to those of other specialists who had been presented with this problem. The others are thought to have included Keldysh and Topchiyev.

It appears that Stalin may have created his own MJ–12-like group (see Chapter 6) to learn what it could from the crash activity in New Mexico. And it can be surmised (in the understandable absence of detailed information) that the initial lead could have come from Soviet spies, some of whom are known to have been in New Mexico in the early post–World War II period.

4

The Search Intensifies

P RIOR TO 1978 reports of crashed alien craft being spirited away by government agents were the substance of science fiction and a few extreme flying saucer magazines. Each report of a crash had died of starvation: Without any form of verification, there was nothing to keep it alive but a few individuals' need to believe. For the vast majority of even those who were convinced that UFOs were real and quite possibly unearthly, the idea that some of them had crashed and been captured was going too far. The subject simply was not worthy of serious discussion.

Then Leonard Stringfield came winging out of Cincinnati to drop his bomb at the July 1978 annual convention of the Mutual UFO Network (MUFON), a nationwide assembly of private UFO investigators, enthusiasts, and hangers-on. This particular meeting was held in Dayton, Ohio, not far from Wright-Patterson Air Force Base, the home of the old Project Blue Book and the scene of so many rumors of alien bodies held in cold storage in the probably mythical Hangar 18. Stringfield's disclosures were made in an unusually tense atmosphere, following a telephoned threat on his life which the local police took seriously enough to warrant a shift in his hotel room and a lot of mysterious scurrying around.

Len had been in the private UFO investigation game for

many years and was best known for his book *Saucer Post 3-0 Blue,* which recounted his experiences as a civilian volunteer in a U.S. Air Force UFO-tracking network. He was regarded as a methodical, reliable investigator who measured his words and protected his sources. He was about to feel the glare of a not-entirely-welcome spotlight.

What distinguished Stringfield from the others who had encountered stories of UFO crashes was his eventual willingness to gather up these orphans who had been rejected by the family of otherwise courageous UFO investigators. Convinced that something of value lay within the hard-to-believe and harder-to-verify crash reports, he went at it with a vengeance.

While writing his second book, *Situation Red, the UFO Siege,* he had begun to focus on rumors of crashes, which he first referred to as Retrievals of the Third Kind and later as simply Crash/Retrievals or just C/R. Publication of the book in 1977 brought additional leads to C/R events, and by 1978 he was ready to go public in a big way.

Stringfield spoke at the Dayton MUFON meeting for two hours, detailing one C/R after another, to the amazement of the hundreds of veteran UFO investigators who had shunned this subcategory of reports prior to the unexpected outpouring of information. Much of the between-lectures chatter centered around Stringfield's revelations, and whether he was unusually perceptive or unusually gullible.

Following his talk, the material was published in amended form in the monthly MUFON journal as a series of abstracts, the purpose being to encourage others to come forth with their own C/R experiences and to feed Len additional information.

The abstracts, discussed:

1. 1948 crash in Mexico, from military sources.
2. 1952 crash in the California desert, which included reports of a damaged UFO being trucked in to Wright-Patterson AFB.
3. 1952 arrival of wreckage at Wright-Patterson AFB, from an ex-guard.

5. 1953 story of an army training film that included footage of a crashed UFO.

6. 1953 crash near Kingman, Arizona, from respected UFO investigator Ray Fowler.

7. 1953 report from a metallurgist taken to an unknown crash site.

8. 1973 Arizona crash story, from a former military pilot.

11. 1953 crash in Montana and the debriefing of civilian witnesses.

12. 1955 report from a woman claiming to have processed sensitive UFO information at Wright-Patterson AFB and then seeing alien bodies there.

13. Undated report of a UFO landing in Arizona that was followed by a fight between aliens and the U.S. military.

14. 1962 New Mexico crash from which two alien bodies were taken to a university medical center for study.

15. A sealed report about crashed UFOs and alien bodies, from an officer who allegedly served for five years in the UFO department at Wright-Patterson AFB.

16. Report of a man said to have guarded alien bodies in Ohio.

18. 1947 crash near Corona, New Mexico

19. 1957 crash in the U.S. Southwest.

Stringfield's published information was admittedly sketchy and unconvincing. There were almost no names or other specifics that could be checked, for he was greatly (perhaps excessively) concerned with protecting the anonymity of his sources. On the face of it, the great revelation was pretty weak: few names, few exact locations or dates. No clear patterns. Only the true believer could hear or read Stringfield's accounts and make more of them than a bunch of disconnected scraps that added up to very little.

Indeed, it wasn't so much the content of Stringfield's disclosures that had an impact as the very existence of so many crash/retrieval reports that set the private UFO investigating field abuzz. It seemed that almost everyone had heard at least one report of a crash but had been unable or unwilling to investigate it for fear of being laughed at and losing hard-won community stature. Now, however, with the cat out of the bag, it was suddenly acceptable to speak openly of crashed flying saucers.

First, however, all this had to be digested, for it carried UFOs into a much more personal and potentially threatening realm. Every private researcher and investigator had to weigh the risks inherent in the dangerous journey into a subject that could easily make him the object of ridicule. But the possible payoff was just too great. If just one crash-and-retrieval could be proved, or even supported by good testimony by individuals willing to be identified publicly, then all the great sightings in anyone's file would be rendered unimportant.

Stringfield had the jump on his fellow investigators, but he was spreading his time and effort over dozens of cases, while others could concentrate on one or two cases and thus stand a chance of getting ahead. Besides, Stringfield was known to be so methodical and cautious that others might well turn his leads into useful information while Len was plodding along.

Among those galvanized into action by the shocking revelations at Dayton was Stanton Friedman. It had been but a few months since his revealing talk with Jesse Marcel, who described recovering strange debris from a sheep ranch. A few months after the Dayton meeting, Friedman talked with Vern Maltais and got the story of Barney Barnett at the Plains of San Augustin. Soon he added confirmation of Marcel's claims in 1947 newspaper stories.

While Stringfield and others were working on their choices of promising leads, Friedman and Bill Moore zeroed in on the Corona, New Mexico, crash, for it was then thought the downed craft seen by Barnett must have been the one that left some of its pieces on the Foster ranch before crashing 150 miles to the west. They had a growing collection of names to check, and many of those named contributed even more names of people to track.

In January 1980 Stringfield privately published his *Status Report II: New Sources, New Data*, which corrected errors in his first report, elaborated on several of his original cases, and added some new ones. Of particular interest was his inclusion of illustrations: of an alien body based on a description from a doctor who claimed to have performed an autopsy; of an alien head from reports given by several alleged witnesses; and of an alien hand which a former CIA employee said was accurately drawn. Like most of his other information, however, there was no way to cross-check any of this.

But others were taking over the vanguard of the search for proof that a UFO had crashed years before, especially the rumors of such activity in New Mexico. In the summer of 1980 *The Roswell Incident* was published. Researched by Bill Moore and Stanton Friedman (who received limited credit in the book and some royalties), and written by Moore and famed travel writer Charles Berlitz, it mixed together what was then known about the crashes at Corona and San Agustin with a lot of extraneous material about UFO sightings by astronauts. The book was generally accurate, but confusingly organized and hard to follow.

Despite its shortcomings, it spread the news of the probable crash to more and more people, and firmly (though misleadingly) established Roswell as the center of crash activity. Friedman and Moore continued to track down and interview witnesses and periodically wrote papers recounting their progress.

Len Stringfield, too, continued to collect and try to check out additional bits of information, publishing his second collection of anecdotes while *The Roswell Incident* was at the publisher, and then a third white paper in June 1982. The New Mexico-centered investigation kept getting deeper and more focused, while Stringfield's was getting broader but no deeper.

Interest remained high during the second half of the 1980s, with two more white papers from Stringfield and more reports by Friedman and Moore published in the formal proceedings of the annual MUFON symposia. Their work on the New Mexico crash or crashes was concentrated and thus cumulative: As the testimony piled up, the credibility of the case grew. Stringfield, on the other hand, continued to make the point that there could be a dozen or more crashes, yet did little in-depth investigation, and so his cases remained vague and inconclusive. He continued to report that his flow of information from informants was subject to abrupt changes: After a period of intense activity it all stopped, as if someone were orchestrating the flow. But nothing was offered as solid evidence of this presumably governmental interference.

In July 1989, during the MUFON symposium in Las Vegas, Nevada, Bill Moore startled the large crowd by admitting to having cooperated with a government disinformation campaign by observing its damaging impact on a witness. His reputation as a source of reliable information suffered, as did his ability to contribute to UFO research. Whose side was he on? Was some of the information Moore published actually disinformation? His direct involvement with the widely panned *UFO Cover-Up, Live!* TV special detracted further from his reputation. Stanton Friedman had no choice but to face this unfortunate situation and disengage himself from the once-productive relationship with Moore and his partner, Jaime Shandera.

In September 1989, the NBC-TV series *Unsolved Mysteries* led off its new season with a half-hour reenactment of the Corona crash, hiring Friedman as a technical adviser and on-camera expert. The show, which was more accurate than the genre referred to as tabloid TV depicted the crash scenes and alien bodies in a nonsensational fashion and drew one of the highest ratings of the week. When repeated the following January, it was again one of the week's top twenty shows. Tens of millions saw the two programs, and scores of them called a special telephone number to offer assistance.

From the many calls recorded, a few provided meaningful leads to persons who had been involved in both the Corona and San Augustin crashes and their aftermaths.

5

The Canadian Connection

L EADS rarely fall into place by themselves. They must be jiggled and turned and rearranged and frequently set aside until some intermediate pieces can be found and fitted. In the search for the pieces of the New Mexico crash puzzle, there have always been far more disjointed bits waiting to be recognized and neatly tucked into place than there were firmly emplaced ones. In fact, the process has been a lot like trying to assemble a blank jigsaw puzzle of unknown size and shape in a room illuminated by a single forty-watt bulb.

One especially important piece of the crash puzzle sat around for years before anyone was able to figure out where it fit. The piece came from the Canadian government, an unlikely source of UFO information.

In 1979, Stanton Friedman was shown a formerly top-secret memorandum by Canadian investigator Scott Foster. It had been sent to the Controller of Telecommunications of the Canadian Department of Transport by Wilbert B. Smith, a senior radio engineer who was working on geomagnetism. The startling portion of the November 21, 1950, memo (which may have been released accidentally) read:

I made discreet inquiries through the Canadian Embassy staff in Washington who were able to obtain for me the following information:

a. The matter is the most highly classified subject in the United States Government, rating even higher than the H-bomb.
b. Flying saucers exist.
c. Their modus operandi is unknown but concentrated effort is being made by a small group headed by Doctor Vannevar Bush.
d. The entire matter is considered by the United States authorities to be of tremendous significance.

What, if anything, did this mean? Smith was known to have had a strong interest in UFOs and had corresponded extensively on the subject with Donald Keyhoe and NICAP. In the late 1950s and early 1960s, Smith exhibited growing signs of mental disturbance blamed on the brain tumor that was to take his life in 1962. But through most of the 1950s he was considered a highly qualified engineer who explored a number of unconventional concepts involving gravity and electromagnetism. Smith was awarded the Canadian Engineering Award posthumously for "Dedicated service in the advancement of the technical standards in Canadian broadcasting."

If what Smith wrote was true, then it was the most important UFO-related government information yet seen. Arthur Bray received the memo from the Canadian government in 1978 (again, possibly by accident) and was eventually able to track down the son of Wilbert Smith and read Smith's handwritten notes on the September 12, 1950, meeting.

Notes on interview through Lt/C. Bremner with Dr. Robert Sarbacher.

SMITH: I am doing some work on the collapse of the earth's magnetic field as a source of energy, and I think our work may have a bearing on the flying saucers.
SARBACHER: What do you want to know?

SMITH: I have read [Frank] Scully's book on the saucers [*Behind the Flying Saucers*] and would like to know how much of it is true.

SARBACHER: The facts reported in the book are substantially correct.

SMITH: Then the saucers do exist?

SARBACHER: Yes, they exist.

SMITH: Do they operate as Scully suggests, on magnetic principles?

SARBACHER: We have not been able to duplicate their performance.

SMITH: Do they come from some other planet?

SARBACHER: All we know is, we didn't make them, and it's pretty certain they didn't originate on the earth.

SMITH: I understand the whole subject of saucers is classified.

SARBACHER: Yes, it is classified two points higher even than the H-bomb. In fact it is the most highly classified subject in the U.S. Government at the present time.

SMITH: May I ask the reason for the classification?

SARBACHER: You may ask, but I can't tell you.

SMITH: Is there any way in which I can get more information, particularly as it might fit in with our own work?

SARBACHER: I suppose you could be cleared through your own Defense Department and I am pretty sure arrangements could be made to exchange information. If you have anything to contribute, we would be glad to talk it over, but I can't give you any more at the present time.

Note: The above is written from memory following the interview. I have tried to keep it as nearly verbatim as possible.

If genuine, this would constitute the most impressive and

convincing evidence of UFO reality and of U.S. government complicity yet revealed. But is it genuine? Fortunately, there are names within the notes that can be checked, and since the notes were found in a large collection of Smith's materials and were in his handwriting, it can reasonably be assumed that they were indeed made by Smith.

It wasn't hard to check out "Lt/C. Bremner," who turned out to have been the defense attaché at the Canadian embassy in Washington, just the sort of person to be involved in a meeting of this magnitude. One down, one to go. And that one—Dr. Robert Sarbacher—would turn out to be the most important individual yet connected with the UFO story.

Stanton Friedman, with the cooperation of Arthur Bray, took up the challenge and in 1982 found Dr. Sarbacher in a directory of leading scientists: A consultant to the U.S. Research and Development Board, he had been the dean of the graduate school at Georgia Tech and was operating his own scientific laboratory, which did some government work.

In the fall of 1983, UFO enthusiast William Steinman had a brief exchange of correspondence with Dr. Sarbacher that produced these answers to his questions:

STEINMAN: Relate your own experience as pertaining to your involvement with these recovered flying saucers—description of saucers, occupants, names of others involved, places of recoveries, dates of recoveries, etc.

SARBACHER: Relating to my own experience regarding flying saucers, I had no association with any of the people involved in the recovery and have no knowledge regarding the dates of the recoveries. If I had I would send it to you.

STEINMAN: Verification that the persons listed were involved: (a) Thomas Townsend Brown; (b) Dr. Weisberg; (c) Dr. Robert H. Kent; (d) Dr. Hellmut Schmidt; (e) Dr. John von Neuman; (f) Dr. Wernher von Braun; (g) Dr. Francis Bitter; (h) Dr. Leo A. GeBauer; (i) Dr. J. Robert

Oppenheimer; (j) Dr. Eric Henry Wang; (k) Dr. Vannevar Bush.

SARBACHER: Regarding verification that persons you list were involved, I can only say this: John von Neuman was definitely involved. Dr. Vannevar Bush was definitely involved, and I think Dr. Robert Oppenheimer also. My association with the Research and Development Board under Dr. Compton during the Eisenhower administration was rather limited so that although I had been invited to participate in several discussions associated with the reported recoveries, I could not personally attend the meetings. I am sure that they would have asked Dr. von Braun, and the others that you listed were probably asked and may or may not have attended. That is all I know for sure.

STEINMAN: A copy of the official Govt. report pertaining to the Aztec, New Mexico recovery [a particular interest of Steinman, though not highly regarded by others], or any other that you might have access to.

SARBACHER: I did receive some official reports when I was in my office at the Pentagon, but all of these were left there as at the time we were never supposed to take them out of the office.

STEINMAN: Copies of the photographs of the recovered flying saucers both at the "Crash-Site" and at the laboratory, and photographs of the occupants of these flying saucers.

SARBACHER: I do not recall receiving any photographs such as you request, so I am not in a position to answer.

STEINMAN: Copies of the official analysis reports both on the saucers and the occupants.

SARBACHER: I have to make the same reply as on [the previous request]. I recall the interview with Dr. Brenner [sic] of the Canadian Embassy. I think the answers I gave him were the ones you listed. Naturally, I was more familiar with the subject matter under discussion at that time. Actually, I would have been able to

give more specific answers had I attended the meetings concerning the subject. You must understand
that I took this assignment as a private contribution.
We were called "dollar-a-year men." My first responsibility was the maintenance of my own business activity so that my participation was limited.

About the only thing I remember at this time is that
certain materials reported to have come from flying
saucer crashes were extremely light and very tough. I
am sure our laboratories analyzed them very carefully.

There were reports that instruments or people operating these machines were also of very light weight,
sufficient to withstand the tremendous deceleration
and acceleration associated with their machinery. I
remember in talking with some of the people at the
office that I got the impression these "aliens" were
constructed like certain insects we have observed on
earth, wherein because of the low mass the inertial
forces involved in operation of these instruments
would be quite low.

I still do not know why the high order of classification has been given and why the denial of the existence of these devices.

In early December 1983, Stanton Friedman called Dr. Sarbacher and was assured that much of the information reported
by Steinman was accurate. He also learned that Sarbacher had
moved at a very high level in the government and knew many
important people. It was therefore logical that he would have
been exposed to such sensitive information.

A further contact with him was made in 1985 by Dr. Bruce
Maccabee, a U.S. Navy physicist who heads the Fund for UFO
Research. Dr. Sarbacher told him "There is something I should
have done but didn't do. I had a request to visit a site [Maccabee
notes: He thinks the request came from Wright Field or that
the site was Wright Field] regarding a fallen UFO and at that
time could not go, [being] tied up with personal business. But

some of the men did go. I went to the office [of the Research and Development Board] some time after they got back and talked to some of the guys who saw it. I wish I could have gone."

Maccabee asked him to relate his impression of what the men told him they saw. "My impression of what the men said who took the trip to Wright Field: the 'people' who operated those things were built different than we. They seemed to have no inertia, seemed to be like insects, maybe they were robots [Maccabee's note: This seemed to stick particularly in his mind].

While no "smoking gun" resulted from the exchanges with Dr. Sarbacher (who died in 1986), his credentials were verified, and thus the amazing memo by Wilbert Smith was given great credibility. Clearly, wreckage and probably bodies were at Wright Field in the early 1950s. Sarbacher told Friedman in a face-to-face meeting in 1983 that there could have been several crashes and that he did not know which crash had produced the materials seen by his associates.

The value of the testimony by Sarbacher and Smith is in the substantiating of rumors of the involvement of Wright Field as a place where materials and/or bodies were located, at least temporarily. Even though Dr. Sarbacher was not able to add a great deal of detail, his stature makes the confirmation of government knowledge of crashed UFOs more impressive than any previous testimony.

A key bit of information was the first mention of Dr. Vannevar Bush in connection with UFOs. While investigating him, Friedman discovered that Bush was the common link among the groups named in the secret (not top secret) September 23, 1947, memo from Gen. Nathan Twining that listed those to which copies of the best saucer information should be sent. These included the Joint Research and Development Board and its predecessor, the Office of Scientific Research and Development (Bush headed both and was thus close to the development of the atomic bomb, proximity fuse, and other major projects); the National Advisory Committee on Aeronautics (Bush had been chairman of this NASA predecessor); and the

Atomic Energy Commission, postwar successor to the Manhattan Project.

Vannevar Bush had easy access to the White House during the war, serving as he did on many vital committees. Thus he would have been in the right place to take a major part in the analysis of saucer wreckage and bodies. These and other groups (such as the Air Force Scientific Advisory Board and the Rand Corporation) were not concerned with day-to-day defense activities, but rather with long-term scientific work. They were just the groups to which one would turn upon finding the remains of a crashed saucer.

6

Majestic-12

MAJESTIC-12 is quite possibly the single most important key to the entire UFO mystery. Except that it has yet to be positively determined that there is a door into which the key fits. Or if this is the correct key to open a very important door.

On the face of it, Majestic-12 (or MAJIC 12 or MJ-12) is a supersecret group of extremely important people from the scientific, military, and intelligence fields who were/are charged with the awesome responsibility of learning everything about what crashed in New Mexico in 1947. If such a group indeed exists (or ever did exist and perhaps was replaced by another group or another designation), it holds more vital secrets than most people can imagine.

If, on the other hand, Majestic-12 never existed, then another group with about the same functions almost certainly did/does. Any alternative to this would mean the U.S. government did not view the New Mexico crashes as important enough to warrant establishing a Majestic-12 by any name. It is difficult to accept the idea that the recovery of unknown materials and the bodies of small humanoids would not be seen in Washington as the scientific/intelligence watershed of the millennium.

The only other possibility is that the crashes never happened, and thus the Majestic-12 documents would have to be part of a hoax. The chances of this being the case have decreased almost to zero, and so the possibility that the documents were created out of whole cloth seems minimal.

The story of Majestic-12 emerged from the catacombs of the U.S. Intelligence community (including the CIA, NSA, FBI, Defense Intelligence Agency, National Reconnaissance Office, and a few other intensely inconspicuous operations), in December 1984, in a manner guaranteed to create suspicion. It arrived in a plain envelope having no return address but an Albuquerque, New Mexico, postmark in the form of a can of exposed-but-unprocessed black-and-white 35mm film.

The innocuous-looking package arrived at the home of Los Angeles movie producer Jaime Shandera, who was known to be working with UFO investigator Bill Moore in intelligence-related activities. When developed and printed, the film revealed eight pages of a purported briefing paper for president-elect Dwight Eisenhower, dated November 18, 1952. It described the discovery, recovery, and preliminary analysis of the remains of what crashed seventy-five miles northwest of Roswell, New Mexico.

Moore and Shandera, together with Stanton Friedman, spent the next two years trying to determine if the document was genuine or phony. Subtle clues and mysterious messages from a growing collection of intelligence (or disinformation) contacts led to furtive phone calls and meetings, but not to much of substance that would enable them to state with confidence that the Eisenhower briefing paper was real. By the spring of 1987, the matter remained as puzzling and inconclusive as ever.

Under circumstances not yet clear, another copy of the document was sent to English UFO writer Timothy Good, engaged in preparing a book about governmental involvement with UFOs. He received his copy in March 1987 and included it in his *Above Top Secret*, published in England in May. By then, Moore and Shandera had released a preliminary version of their document, in an unfortunately abbreviated and censored form, with the original security classification words crossed out in quasi-official style (by Moore, as it turned out).

At the MUFON symposium at American University in Washington, D.C., in June 1987, the full document was released by Moore and company. But as verification was still lacking, this kicked off a flurry of rumors, denials, and accusations.

Before the meaning and the importance of the Eisenhower briefing paper can be judged, it first must be shown that it is genuine, and that has so far proved extremely difficult. Simply asking the appropriate people in the government if it is real would seem to be the logical way to find out. Failing this, a request under the useful provisions of the Freedom of Information Act would be in order. But any document as highly classified as this one appears to be on its face would be known to but a few especially trustworthy individuals who could be counted on to keep their mouths shut about it. The Freedom of Information Act, as effective as it can be, does not provide entree to highly classified information whose very existence is easy to deny and all but impossible to prove.

If the Eisenhower briefing paper is an officially approved hoax, finding the person or office responsible for its creation and then extracting a confession would be next to impossible. It would therefore appear that keeping the document from being proved either genuine or fake is all but guaranteed. It is certain to remain controversial until someone comes forth with proof, one way or the other.

The immediate reaction to the emergence of the document, from several factions—both pro- and anti-UFO reality—was to declare it a hoax, even a "proven hoax." Alleged discrepancies in the form, or the typeface, or the official jargon claimed to have been standard in 1952 were trumpeted as proof that it had been concocted by unknown parties for purposes never made quite clear. Proponents of the paper's validity, along with others not ready to condemn it as a fake on the basis of somewhat flimsy evidence, set to work to find out all they could about the document, without any great expectations of arriving at a final answer.

What is very clear is that whoever composed the Eisenhower briefing paper, be he a legitimate part of an MJ-12, a vintage hoaxer or a recent one, knew a great deal about UFO history, about the crash near Corona, and about the inner workings of the U.S. government, including the backgrounds and activities of the twelve men alleged to have been the original members of Majestic-12. It could hardly be just another crude hoax perpetrated by some wag with an old typewriter, like several that had bedeviled the private UFO community over the years. It had taken a lot of research and checking and probably prior hoaxing experience, and thus must be very important to its originator, rather than a mere prank.

But why go to all this trouble to create a phony document? Was it to embarrass and discredit UFO investigators (thereby reducing their effectiveness) by getting them to accept the document as real and then revealing it as a fake and those who believed it as pathetically gullible? If so, the hoaxer has let a lot of years and a lot of opportunities go by without speaking out. And with each passing year there is the growing likelihood that a claim or admission of hoaxing may not be believed. After all, for someone simply to stand up and announce "Ho ho! I did it and you dummies fell for it!" won't be enough. Proof that it was a hoax will be demanded, and that could prove as elusive as establishing absolute authenticity has so far been.

Was it meant to occupy the time and energy of the best people in the UFO community and thus draw their attention away from some other government UFO event or non-UFO project that was considered more sensitive, or on the verge of being revealed? One has to wonder just what could be more volatile than the discovery of proof that UFOs are alien spacecraft.

More and more, it appears that even if the Eisenhower briefing paper is a hoax, there must be something very similar in existence, since the reality of the Corona crash increases in probability with each passing day. Why fake a document when a real one with substantially similar content may be in the very next filing cabinet?

It is also a possibility that the original purpose of a phony briefing paper has been made obsolete by events subsequent to its creation. It could be hanging in midair without any purpose or any way to get rid of it without causing major embarrassment to possibly innocent parties.

Given the powerful content of the briefing paper, it became imperative to establish its genuineness or falsity as firmly as possible. It was to this purpose that in the summer of 1988 the Fund for UFO Research, Inc., embarked upon a successful campaign to raise $16,000 to support the proposal from Stanton Friedman to investigate the Majestic-12 documents (by then there were more than one), with the goal of establishing their basic nature.

Analyzing the primary document presented Friedman with several major problems, some of which were the result of his inability to work with the original document. Only a photographic copy was available, and so there was no way to test the paper, the ink or any other physical characteristic. To compound the problem, Moore and Shandera were unwilling to make the photographic negatives of the document available for study, though it is doubtful that much could have been learned from them.

The starting point had to be the best possible copy of the prints made from the negatives—a third-generation version of the original, unfortunately. But the content of the paper could be read with ease, and so this was the closest approximation of original evidence that could be acquired.

The format of the briefing paper got considerable attention. Was it reasonable for the time (1952) and for such a high-level document allegedly prepared for the White House? Were there any serious discrepancies from known practices? Was it the sort of thing that might be expected to have been created under the circumstances?

In a letter to private UFO enthusiast Lee Graham, former CIA official Richard Bissell, who headed up the U-2 and Bay of Pigs operations, said: "The document certainly looks authentic. On the basis of the material you have sent me, I personally have little doubt that it is authentic." Similar testimonials to the apparent authenticity of the Eisenhower briefing paper have been received by Friedman from Truman administrative assistant David Stowe and from one-time National Security Council planning board member Robert R. Bowie. (The document appears in the Appendices.)

The date format in the middle of the cover sheet also got great attention: 18 November, 1952. Is it correct to have a comma between the month and the year, or is this evidence of fraud? Present government practice dictates no comma, but in the early 1950s there were many different date formats in use within the White House. Several like the one in question have been found on official presidential documents and related papers whose authenticity has never been questioned. Only when computers and word processors came into common use did date format became consistent. Moreover, a sophisticated hoaxer would probably have used a more common style in order not to draw attention to the date format.

The security classification: TOP SECRET/MAJIC National Security Information Eyes Only. Does it make sense? The only unfamiliar word is MAJIC, which can be assumed to be a code word that limits access to persons cleared specifically for information on this subject. This means that only those few individuals having a specific "need to know" about MJ-12 would be allowed to read it, rather than anyone cleared for top secret, which runs to many hundreds of thousands of employees of the military, other government agencies, and private contractors engaged in sensitive work.

Regarding the writing style of the entire document: Does it fit other material known to have been written by Adm. Roscoe Hillenkoetter, who is identified on page two as the briefing officer? Actually, there is no reason it should, as there is no evidence that it was written personally by Hillenkoetter, who could easily have roughed it out and then given it to someone else for final writing. In that case, it would not have represented the writing style of Hillenkoetter, yet it would be an accurate statement of his position.

However, in order to determine if the briefing paper fit Hillenkoetter's style, it was presented to world-famous linguistics expert Dr. Roger W. Wescott, of Drew University in New Jersey, along with more than twenty examples of notes and memos known to have been written by Hillenkoetter. After studying them, Wescott wrote: "In my opinion, there is no compelling reason to regard any of these communications as fraudulent or to believe that any of them were written by anyone other than Hillenkoetter himself. This statement holds for the controversial presidential briefing memorandum of November 18, 1952, as well as for the letters, both official and personal."

This, of course, does not prove that the Eisenhower briefing paper was written by Admiral Hillenkoetter. It only means that an expert found no evidence of fraud. Even if there were evidence that it was not written by Hillenkoetter, this would not necessarily mean it was a fake, only that the text was not prepared directly by him. It is certainly possible that an inspection of the original document would produce evidence of the use of modern paper or ink . . . or that it would produce evidence of the use of paper and ink appropriate to 1952. These matters remain unsettled.

It has been suggested that listing Admiral Hillenkoetter as Roscoe rather than by his initials, R. H., is strong evidence (some actually insist it is proof) the paper is a fake because he is said to have hated that name and always used his initials. Testimony by his widow and by close friends agrees that he frequently used "Roscoe" and in fact was generally known by that name.

The content of the briefing paper offers the greatest opportunity for checking, and that is where most of the effort has gone, starting with the members of the Majestic-12 group. If they were the sort of men who had the knowledge and abilities, the experience and connections needed for such a novel, sensitive, and important assignment, then one can assume that either the document is real or was written by someone with suspiciously complete access to the needed information.

MEMBERS OF THE MJ-12 GROUP

The following very brief backgrounds of the twelve men said to have been members of MJ-12 include their positions at the time of the formation of MJ-12 in 1947 (boldface type).

REAR ADMIRAL ROSCOE H. HILLENKOETTER. First **Director of the Central Intelligence Agency** (1947–1950).

DR. VANNEVAR BUSH. Chairman of the National Defense Research Commission and Office of Scientific Research and Development during World War II. Chairman of the National Advisory Committee on Aeronautics (NACA, later NASA), 1939–1941. **Chairman of the Joint Research and Development Board** (1945–1948).

JAMES V. FORRESTAL. Secretary of the Navy, 1945–1947. First **Secretary of Defense**, 1947–1949.

GEN. NATHAN F. TWINING. **Commander of the USAAF Air Materiel Command, Wright Field**, 1945–1947.

GEN. HOYT VANDENBERG. Chief of Military Intelligence for the War Department during World War II. Second Director of Central Intelligence, 1946–1947. **Chief of the Air Staff**, 1947. Chief of Staff of the U.S. Air Force, 1948–1953.

DR. DETLEV BRONK. Founder of the science of biophysics. Member of the Scientific Advisory Committee of the Brookhaven National Laboratories. **Chairman of the National Research Council**, 1946–1950. President of the National Academy of Sciences, 1950–1962. President of Johns Hopkins University.

DR. JEROME HUNSAKER. Chairman of the Departments of Aeronautical and Mechanical Engineering of the Massachusetts Institute of Technology, 1933–1951. **Chairman of NACA**, 1941–1956.

SIDNEY SOUERS. First Director of Central Intelligence, 1946. First **Executive Secretary of the National Security Council**, 1947–1950. Special consultant on intelligence matters to President Harry Truman.

GORDON GRAY. **Assistant Secretary of the Army**, 1947–1949. Secretary of the Army, 1949–1950. Chairman of the CIA's hush-hush Psychological Strategy Board.

DONALD MENZEL. Professor of astrophysics, Harvard University, 1939–1971. **Chairman, Department of Astronomy**, 1946–1949.

LLOYD V. BERKNER. **Executive Secretary of the Research and Development Board**, 1946–1947. Recipient of the Congressional Gold Medal.

MAJ. GEN. ROBERT M. MONTAGUE. **Commanding Officer of the area that included the White Sands Proving Ground**, 1946–1947. Appointed head of a classified project at Sandia Base, New Mexico, immediately after the crash.

These men represented the very cream of the American military, intelligence, and scientific communities in the summer of 1947. All were perfectly logical and obvious choices for such an unusual and important project. All, that is, except for Donald Menzel, best known for three books in which he ridiculed UFOs and those who took them seriously. He was recognized as the leading anti-UFO spokesman of American science and as such influenced a generation of opinion-makers.

Menzel's involvement with such a government operation had never been hinted at during his many years of anti-UFO tirades. Was his inclusion in the MJ-12 group a slip-up on the part of some unknown and possibly playful hoaxer? Or were there things about Donald Menzel not generally known?

Extensive research by Stanton Friedman in previously untouched and hard-to-get-to Menzel papers at Harvard revealed an entire "second life" for the nationally known scientist. He had been deeply involved in high-level covert CIA and National Security Agency operations for many years, including work in the code-breaking field and many other highly classified assignments never suspected even by his widow and his closest associates at Harvard. But those who knew him best agreed that he was fully capable of keeping secrets—he would actually have enjoyed leading a double life—and so could well have been involved in all sorts of "black" activities. He kept all knowledge of this to himself even during the McCarthy-style loyalty/security hearings in 1950 which threatened to remove his Air Force Secret clearance for having led a scientific expedition to the U.S.S.R. in 1936—even though he had a rare Top Secret-Ultra clearance that far superseded it.

Of particular interest is the effort demanded of Friedman to acquire this previously unknown information. It required permission from two Harvard department heads and Mrs. Menzel. If the hoax had been perpetrated by someone within the government, it would have to have been by someone with access to the most sensitive information. Not impossible, but highly unlikely, and thus evidence of the great and unexplained importance of such a hoax.

While the members of the MJ-12 group were the sort deserving of being on such a panel, did they behave as if they really were involved in this? Stanton Friedman tracked them down (the last of the twelve to die was Jerome Hunsaker—in 1984, shortly before the Eisenhower briefing paper surfaced) through telephone and appointment logs, and personal and official correspondence found in their papers in presidential libraries and the documents division of the Library of Congress. Their comings and goings, their meetings and conferences could be traced on certain significant dates.

One of the attachments to the Eisenhower briefing paper— the only one that accompanied the document—is a memo from President Truman to Secretary of Defense Forrestal dated September 24, 1947, telling Forrestal of the establishment of MJ-12 and referring to a recent conversation between the two of them on this matter. September 24 was the only day between May and December 1947 on which Truman and Vannevar Bush met, and thus was the likely time for the decision to create MJ-12. Bush and Forrestal, the two men credited in the briefing paper as having recommended the establishment of MJ-12, met on that day as well and saw Truman together. No prankster could possibly have known this: it took Friedman many, many hours and thousands of miles of travel to discover these facts.

In addition, September 24 was the day after Gen. Nathan Twining wrote his report on what was known about the flight characteristics of "flying saucers." What better time to take action by establishing a formal group to investigate sighting reports as well as crashes? Twining, according to his and his pilot's flight logs had flown to Alamagordo Army Air Field, New Mexico, on July 7, 1947, remaining in the state (with a side trip to Kirtland Air Force Base, Albuquerque) until July 11 before returning to Wright Field. In a July 17 letter to an executive of the Boeing Airplane Co. Twining wrote: "With deepest regrets we had to cancel our trip to the Boeing factory due to a very important and sudden matter that developed here." Could he have been in New Mexico in connection with the crash?

CONTENT OF THE EISENHOWER BRIEFING PAPER

Since there is obviously reason to believe (though perhaps not to accept completely) that the document is real, its content assumes considerable potential importance. If it fits what is known and what is reasonable, the chances of its legitimacy improve, as does its significance.

The first paragraph of the text of the briefing paper describes the UFO situation prior to the New Mexico crash and fits what has long been known about the first rash of American "flying saucer" sightings in late June and early July 1947. But one has to wonder about the basis for the statement "Public reaction bordered on near hysteria at times." Most people reacted to the reports of saucer-shaped things scooting across the sky with laughter, not with hysteria or even near-hysteria. Perhaps someone was trying to take credit for preventing a panic within the government, if not out in public.

Other statements in the first paragraph refer to alleged events that are even less well known. If there were "independent efforts by several different elements of the military to ascertain the nature and purpose of these objects in the interests of national defense," only that by the Air Materiel Command has ever been mentioned before. Who else was so concerned about the reports? The navy? The marines? The cavalry? Or maybe other groups within the USAAF? Also, what is behind the words "there were several unsuccessful attempts to utilize aircraft in efforts to pursue reported discs in flight"? Attempts to intercept UFOs in the early days have never been made public, though they make sense, and the classic bureaucratese in which this was written suggests its author had spent considerable time in the government.

The second paragraph refers to the discovery of a crashed saucer on a remote ranch in New Mexico and fits very neatly with what has been learned from other sources.

The third paragraph continues to fit the increasingly complete knowledge of the aftermath of the discovery of the wreckage. That a secret operation to recover the wreckage was begun on July 7 or 8 is well established. And the finding of the bodies of several "small human-like beings" some distance from the Brazel ranch fits with what is now known of the claims of several witnesses.

The length of time the bodies were said to have lain out in the open conforms to the latest chronology of the crash: "approximately one week" is the time between the crash on July 2 and the most likely day of the discovery of the bodies by the main military search team involved in the recovery. It is reasonable that the bodies had by then undergone considerable decomposition by the elements, and perhaps further damage by predators.

Removal of the bodies and wreckage can be traced to some extent, though evidence that wreckage was "removed to several different locations" has only recently come to light. The "debriefing" of civilian and military witnesses is hardly surprising, especially in light of the testimony that rancher Brazel was held incommunicado by the army for a week, during and after which he "agreed" with them that the wreckage was mundane. The "weather balloon" cover story has been testified to by several ex-military people who have since admitted to being aware that it was phony.

Page four concerns highly classified efforts to learn the nature of the wreckage and bodies, all of which is perfectly logi-cal, but never detailed until the briefing paper was leaked. It is interesting that Dr. Menzel is mentioned as having been in-volved in the question of the origin of the craft (as an astro-physicist, he would be the first choice) but not in the attempt to decipher the symbols found on parts of the wreckage. His knowledge of cryptanalysis and of Japanese, a symbolic lan-guage, should have made him an obvious choice for this diffi-cult task.

The confusion at finding no evidence of metal wiring, which was the only known form of electrical connection and trans-mission in 1947, is understandable. Solid-state electronics arose *after* the crashes, with the late-1947 invention of the transistor. That this now-common device might have resulted from study of the wreckage has been suggested by scientists with knowledge of these events, and the plausibility of this connection is supported by histories of science that point to the relatively sudden invention of the transistor shortly after the date of the crashes.

On page five, the briefing goes into the formation of an official government UFO investigation—initially Project Sign—though its suggested purpose was to pass along informa-tion about UFOs, their performance, and their functions to MJ-12, rather than to determine if they were a threat to the national security, as the public was repeatedly told. To do this, a secret liaison system was set up between the project and MJ-12, using a "mole" in the investigation who often, if not always, was the project director. While no mention of this is made in any of former project director Ed Ruppelt's writings, his orders could easily have been too highly classified to per-mit that, and he may not have known exactly where his infor-mation was going, or why.

The discovery of a second crashed object on December 6, 1950, fits what is known about some very mysterious activ-ities around that time. A high state of alert was noted in several books about the Truman administration, Truman's memoirs and papers in his library, and even an FBI teletype message about an Army Intelligence alert for "any data whatsoever concerning flying saucers." This reported crash has yet to be properly investigated by private UFO groups.

The final paragraph on page five mentions the increased level of UFO activity in the spring and summer of 1952—the huge sighting wave centered on Washington, D.C. However, the activity had returned to normal levels (four to five per week) well before the briefing paper was delivered, and so the obvious concern is a sign that the Pentagon was highly disturbed by the flap. Hence it is pointed to as the basis for increased security in order to prevent panic, as well as for unspecified "international and technological considerations." A contingency plan dated January 31, 1949 (a year and a half after the crash), was put in place "should the need to make a public announcement present itself." Just what would constitute justification for a public release of information is not even hinted at, though one can guess that a landing or a crash observed by many people (or even TV cameras) might be the sort of event that would override all plans for keeping the news under wraps.

The seven attachments not included with the leaked document (or made available later by the high-level informants of Moore and Shandera) must contain a world of vital information. They cover such matters as the analyses of the wreckage, bodies and symbols.

RELATED DOCUMENTS

Easily the most controversial of all the MJ-12–related materials is usually referred to as the Cutler–Twining memo. It allegedly was sent from Robert Cutler, a special assistant to President Eisenhower, to Lt. Gen. Nathan Twining. It appears to concern the rescheduling of a Majestic-12 Special Studies Project (MJ-12 SSP) meeting on July 16, 1954.

The controversy revolves around the manner in which the document was discovered. William Moore and Jaime Shandera found it in 1985 while searching through more than a hundred boxes of recently declassified documents in Records Group 341 (RG 341) at the National Archives in Washington. The memo was found between two folders and is a White House document completely unrelated to RG 341, which is composed of Air Force material. It was found in box number 189, which had been hinted at in a mysterious postcard received by Moore from New Zealand with a return address of Box 189, Addis Ababa, Ethiopia, though the significance of the box number did not register until after the fact.

It would appear that the Cutler–Twining memo was planted in RG 341, Box 189 by someone who wanted it to be found. But who planted it is unknown, since the only people with access to the material were National Archives employees and the Air Force people who declassified the thousands of pages in RG 341. It is highly unlikely that anyone else could have done it, as the means of access to such material is carefully controlled by the security-conscious National Archives staff.

The memo is obviously a carbon copy, on a type of onionskin paper manufactured in limited and controlled quantities between 1953 and the early 1970s, and is discolored around the edges as would be expected of an old piece of paper. The lack of Cutler's signature has been the target of attacks on the validity of the memo. There isn't even a typed "/s/," which would indicate that the original was signed. Investigation by Friedman revealed that Robert Cutler was out of the country on the day the memo was written, so an aide must have prepared it— as aides prepared many other memos and letters in those days. The lack of a signature therefore is not evidence of its fabrication; indeed, had it carried a signature when Cutler was away, there would be solid reason to be suspicious.

A July 3, 1954, memo was found by Friedman at the Eisenhower Library in which Cutler instructed James Lay, executive secretary of the National Security Council, to "Keep things moving out of my basket." Another memo, written on July 16, reveals Lay telling Cutler: "Hope you will recuperate, rest and enjoy yourself for the days before returning. Will try to have everything tidy and not too much pressure on you when you arrive." Clearly, Lay was taking care of routine matters during Cutler's absence.

The final answer to the question of the legitimacy of the

MJ-12 documents is not yet in. Those who reacted most negatively to its initial release remain convinced it is a fake, while those who think it is real have no proof. One of the arguments for the doubtful character of the Eisenhower briefing paper is its lack of reference to the crash at the Plains of San Agustin. One possible explanation for this is that the briefing paper could be a copy of most of the original, with the copier omitting any reference to the second crash because, at the time, this had been given only limited credence. In this way, the briefing paper could well be both genuine and fake: genuine in its content but a copy made any time after 1947. Admittedly, this is pure speculation.

Lt. Walter Haut, the Public Information Officer at Roswell Army Air Field, who issued the press release that told of the Army's recovery of a crashed flying disc in 1947 (*photo courtesy of Walter Haut*).

Col. William "Butch" Blanchard, commanding officer of the 509th Bomb Group at Roswell Army Air Field, who ordered Lt. Haut to issue the press release (*photo courtesy of Smithsonian Institute*).

Col. Thomas J. Dubose, chief of staff of the 8th Air Force and the man who was ordered to invent a cover story for the Corona crash (*photo courtesy of Smithsonian Institute*).

BELOW LEFT: Brigadier General Ramey, commanding officer of the 8th Air Force at Ft. Worth Army Air Field, 1947, who told the press that the material recovered from the Foster ranch was just the remains of the radar reflector of a weather balloon (*photo courtesy of Smithsonian Institute*).

BELOW RIGHT: Major Jesse Marcel, as a Lieutenant during World War II (*photo courtesy of Dr. Jesse Marcel*).

Out building on the Foster ranch where Maj. Marcel and CIC man
Cavitt bunked overnight before seeing the debris field with "Mac"
Brazel.

Wright Field (later named Wright Patterson Air Force Base) in late
1945. It looked the same in July, 1947, when some of the wreckage
from the Corona crash was flown there (*photo courtesy of Smithsonian Institute*).

Glenn Dennis, former mortician at Roswell in 1947, at right; Walter Haut stands next to him (*photo courtesy Walter Haut*).

Rear of the hospital at Roswell Army Air Field. It was here that Glenn Dennis parked and walked in while small humanoid bodies were being prepared for shipment.

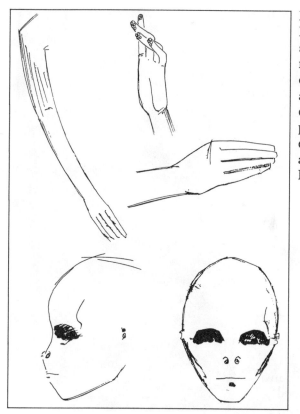

Drawings by Glenn Davis, based on the sketches by his nurse friend on the day after she assisted two doctors in the preliminary examination of alien bodies at Roswell.

Dr. Jesse Marcel standing next to the Army helicopter he flies as a colonel in the Reserves (*photo courtesy Dr. Jesse Marcel*).

Grady "Barney" Barnett, who was among those who discovered the crash site in the Plains of San Agustin (*photo courtesy Alice Knight*).

BELOW: The plains of San Agustin where a second UFO crashed in 1947.

Jerry Anderson at the Plains of San Agustin in 1990.

Anderson describes his memories of the 1947 crash site to author Stanton Friedman.

Stanton Friedman, Jerry Anderson, hypnotist John Carpenter, and financial backer Robert Bigelow at San Agustin in 1990.

7

Civilians Find the Wreckage

I T ALL BEGAN on the morning of Thursday, July 3, 1947, when two innocent people stumbled upon the remains of a crashed "flying disc" on a section of sheep ranch dotted with rocks, scrub bushes, and tough buffalo grass. William "Mac" Brazel, foreman of Foster Ranch, and his 7-year-old neighbor Dee Proctor were out checking for damage after the previous night's violent thunderstorm.

Sometime during the previous evening, they had heard a "different" crash among the many claps of thunder. No damage to fences or windmills could be found, but something quite unexpected arrested their attention: a field full of bits and pieces of shiny material unlike anything the veteran rancher had ever seen.

According to newspaper reports at the time, Mac gathered some of it up and hid it under a bush or in a shed. He kept a few pieces, one of which he took with him when he drove Dee the few miles back to the home of his parents, Floyd and Loretta Proctor, his nearest neighbors. The boy had been with Mac because he loved riding horses above all else, and this was what Mac did much of the time.

In July 1990, Loretta Proctor was interviewed during a special conference on crashes held by the Fund for UFO Research in Washington. And since both Mac and her husband had died long before anyone got on the trail of the crash mystery, she was the most direct link to the beginning of the story. Loretta is a wonderful example of a Western ranch lady: open, hospitable, and not the least interested in publicity that might compromise the solitary life she leads in an old ranchhouse at the end of a hilly dirt road.

[Mac] had this piece of material that he had picked up. He wanted to show it to us and wanted us to go down and see the rest of the debris or whatever, [but] we didn't on account of the transportation and everything wasn't too good. He didn't get anybody to come out who was interested in it. The piece he brought looked like a kind of tan, light-brown plastic . . . it was very lightweight, like balsa wood. It wasn't a large piece, maybe about four inches long, maybe just a little larger than a pencil.

We cut on it with a knife and would hold a match on it, and it wouldn't burn. We knew it wasn't wood. It was smooth like plastic, it didn't have real sharp corners, kind of like a dowel stick. Kind of dark tan. It didn't have any grain . . . just smooth. I hadn't seen anything like it.

In a series of papers published in the 1980s, Stanton Friedman and Bill Moore reported on interviews with others who had seen and handled bits of the Corona wreckage before the army clamped down:

Mrs. Bessie Brazel Schreiber, Mac Brazel's daughter: The material resembled

a sort of aluminumlike foil. Some of [these] pieces had a sort of tape stuck to them . . . [but] even though the stuff looked like tape, it could not be peeled off or removed at all. Some of these pieces had something like numbers and lettering on them, but there were no words we were able to make out. The figures were written out like you would write numbers in columns . . . but they didn't look like the numbers we use at all.

. . . a piece of something made out of the same metal-like foil that looked like a pipe sleeve. About four inches across and equally long, with a flange on one end. [Also] what appeared to be pieces of a heavily waxed paper.

William Brazel, Mac's son:

... something on the order of tinfoil, except that [it] wouldn't tear. . . . You could wrinkle it and lay it back down and it immediately resumed its original shape . . . quite pliable, but you couldn't crease or bend it like ordinary metal. Almost like a plastic, but definitely metallic. Dad once said that the Army had once told him it was not anything made by us.

[There was also] some threadlike material. It looked like silk . . . but was not silk . . . a very strong material [without] strands or fibers like silk would have. This was more like a wire—all one piece or substance.

. . . some woodenlike particles . . . like balsa wood in weight, but a bit darker in color and much harder. . . . It was pliable but wouldn't break. . . . weighed nothing, but you couldn't scratch it with your fingernail. All I had was a few small bits. [There was no writing or markings on the pieces I had] but Dad did say one time that there were what he called "figures" on some of the pieces he found. He often referred to the petroglyphs the ancient Indians drew on the rocks around here as "figures," too, and I think that's what he meant to compare them with.

Walt Whitmore, Jr., son of the owner of Roswell radio station KGFL: "[It was] very much like lead foil in appearance but could not be torn or cut at all . . . extremely light in weight . . . some small beams that appeared to be either wood or woodlike had a sort of writing on it which looked like numbers which had either been added or multiplied [in columns]."

So far, the only people who knew that something strange had crashed on the Foster Ranch were civilians. Mac Brazel's life was centered on the sheep ranch and, since he was unaware of the "flying saucer" craze sweeping the country, did not connect them with what had scattered pieces across one of his fields. Only after friends had urged him to tell the army about what happened did he drive to Roswell, a formidable trek in those days and one that still involves traveling a lot of miles on unpaved roads.

On Sunday, July 6, Mac showed up at the office of Chaves County Sheriff George Wilcox with a few samples of debris he had picked up from the ranch. The sheriff quickly realized it was something unusual and called Roswell Army Air Field and talked with Major Jesse Marcel, the intelligence officer. Marcel and Sheridan Cavitt of the Counter-Intelligence Corps then drove back to the ranch with Mac to begin the military's involvement with the crash.

When Marcel returned from the ranch with a carload of debris, he stopped at home and rousted his wife and son Jesse out of bed to show them what he had found. As the discovery of strange materials had not yet been declared a classified subject by the army, he was breaking no rule in so doing. The eleven-year-old Jesse, now a successful medical doctor, army reserve helicopter pilot who served in Vietnam, and a qualified aircraft accident investigator, remembers the experience clearly.

> The crash and remnants of the device that I happened to see have left an imprint on my memory that can never be forgotten. The craft was not conventional in any sense of the word, in that the remains were most likely what was then known as a "flying saucer" that had apparently been stressed beyond its designed capabilities.
>
> I'm basing this on the fact that many of the remnants, including I-beam pieces that were present, had strange hieroglyphic typewriting symbols across the inner surfaces . . . pink and purple, except that I don't think there were any animal figures present as there are in true Egyptian hieroglyphics.
>
> The remainder of the debris was just described as nondescript metallic debris, or just shredded fragments, but there was a fair amount of the intact I-beam members present. I only saw a small portion of the debris that was actually present at the crash site.

Sometime before the crash site was sealed off, Sheriff Wilcox appears to have driven out there and seen a lot. In early 1991,

Kevin Randle interviewed Miss Barbara Dugger, granddaughter of George and Inez Wilcox. The sheriff had died when Barbara was quite young, but she lived with her grandmother while going to college and became very close to the elderly but still dynamic Inez Wilcox. According to Barbara:

[My grandmother said] "Don't tell anybody. When the incident happened, the military police came to the jailhouse and told George and I that if we ever told anything about the incident, not only would we be killed, but our entire family would be killed!"

They called my grandfather and someone came and told him about this incident. He went out there to the site; there was a big burned area and he saw debris. It was in the evening. There were four "space beings." Their heads were large. They wore suits like silk. One of the "little men" was alive.

If she said it happened, it happened!

As for the death threat, Barbara's grandmother made it clear: "They meant it, Barbara—they were not kidding!"

"She said the event shocked him. He never wanted to be sheriff again after that. Grandmother ran for sheriff and was defeated. My grandmother was a very loyal citizen of the United States, and she thought it was in the best interest of the country not to talk about it." Inez Wilcox died not long afterward, at the age of ninety-three.

There is a very clear pattern concerning threats to witnesses: Those who saw only wreckage have gotten away lightly, while those who saw bodies were treated much more severely. Since even direct contact with wreckage would not by itself prove the alien nature of the crash, it is understandable that witnesses whose experiences were limited to hardware would not be considered serious threats by the military. But even a brief glimpse of a body would have made it pretty obvious that this was a nonhuman event; it is just as understandable that the government would choose to apply much more drastic pressure to those who had seen bodies.

Members of the local press involuntarily became participants in the drama, rather than merely observers. Frank Joyce of radio station KGFL got a phone call while on duty at the station one afternoon from a man who reported wreckage on his ranch—presumably Mac Brazel.

He asked me what to do about it. I recommended he go to Roswell Army Air Base [sic].

The next thing I heard was that the PIO, [Lt.] Walter Haut, came into the station some time after I got this call. He handed me a news release printed on onionskin stationary and left immediately. I called him back at the base and said, "I suggest that you not release this type of story that says you have a flying saucer or flying disc." He said, "No, it's OK. I have the OK from the C.O. [Colonel Blanchard]."

I sent the release on the Western Union wire to the United Press bureau. After I returned to the station, there was a flash on the wire with the story: "The U.S. Army Air Corps [sic] says it has a flying disc." They typed a paragraph or two, and then other people got on the wire and asked for more information. Then the phone calls started coming on, and I referred them to [the airfield].

Then the wire stopped and just hummed. Then a phone call came in, and the caller identified himself as an officer at the Pentagon, and this man said some very bad things about what would happen to me . . . he was really pretty nasty. Finally, I got through to him: I said, "you're talking about a release from the U.S. Army Air Corps!" Bang! The phone went dead; he was just gone.

Then [station owner Walt] Whitmore called me and said, "Frank, what's going on down there?" He was quite upset. He asked, "Where did you get this story?" In the meantime, I got this [USAAF news] release and hid it, to have proof so no one could accuse me of making it up. Whitmore came in to the station and I gave him the release. He took it with him.

The next significant thing occurred in the evening. I got a call from [Mac] Brazel. He said, "We haven't got this story right." I invited him over to the station; he arrived not long after sunset. He was alone, but I had the feeling that we were being watched. He said something about a weather balloon. I said, "Look, this is completely different than what you told me on the phone the other day about the little green men," and that's when he said, "No, they weren't green." I had the feeling he was under tremendous pressure.

He said, "Our lives will never be the same again."

The other Roswell radio station, KSWS, got into the adventure as well. Some time on Monday, July 7, staff member Johnny McBoyle may have visited the sheep ranch and seen wreckage, if not bodies. While he refuses to discuss the matter even after almost a half century, another principal has been found: Lydia Sleppy, the teletype operator whose message was interrupted so mysteriously. Long thought to have died, she was located by Stanton Friedman in October 1990, and interviewed.

We were Mutual Broadcasting and ABC, and if we had anything newsworthy, we would put it on the [teletype] machine, and I was the one who did the typing. It was in my office. [Station owner] Mr. [Merle] Tucker was in Washington, D.C., trying to get an application approved for a station in El Paso, when this call came from John McBoyle. He told me he had something hot for the network. I said, "Give me a minute and I'll get the assistant manager," because if it was anything like that, I wanted one of them there while I was taking it down.

I went back and asked Mr. [Karl] Lambertz (he came up from the big Dallas station) if he would come up and watch. John was dictating and [Karl] was standing right at my shoulder. I got into it enough to know that it was a pretty big story, when the bell came on [signaling an interruption]. Typing came across: "This is the FBI, you will cease transmitting."

I had my shorthand pad, and I turned around and told [Karl] that I had been cut off, but that I could take it in shorthand and then we could call it in to the network. I took it in shorthand, as John went on to give the story. He had seen them take the thing away . . . he'd been out there [presumably at the Foster ranch] when they took it away. And at that time, if I remember correctly, John said they were gonna load it up and take it to Texas. But when the planes came in, they were from Wright Field.

It isn't known if this happened before Lieutenant Haut distributed his explosive news release about the army recovering the remains of a flying disc or about the same time. But once the news got out, the reaction of the nation's and even the world's press was rapid. For two weeks, it had been full of tales of "routine" flyovers of vaguely described shiny discs and silvery balls. And so this offbeat story of the recovery of actual pieces of one of the things was played for all it was worth.

Suddenly, Roswell, New Mexico, was on the map. The sleepy little Western town, whose main claim to fame as the home of the A-bomb-carrying 509th Bomb Group had long been stifled by military security, was instantly transformed into the world center of . . . something. Phone calls from reporters as far away as London poured into the sheriff's office, the radio stations, newspapers, and of course Roswell Army Air Field. The city fathers reveled in all the attention, while the military shuddered.

Everyone wanted to know more about this earthshaking event: Exactly what was found at the ranch? What was it like? What had been done with it? Could we see it? And especially, was it really the remains of one of those mysterious flying discs?

The afternoon edition of the July 9 Roswell *Daily Record*, which was written well after the mystery had supposedly been solved by the Eighth Air Force, expressed a popular feeling about the episode with this editorial:

AND NOW WHAT IS IT?

With telephones ringing, excited voices shouting into newsroom personnel ears, pouring out eager questions which were unanswerable, it was discovered shortly after publication time of the *Record* yesterday afternoon that curiosity over the reports from 44 states of the union that silver discs had crystallized into belief.

The *Record* had no more than "hit the streets" until the telephone barrage began, with questioners checking up on what they had just read, doubtful of their own eyes.

But the story stood, just as all amazing things stand in these days of wonderful feats and curious performances.

What the disk is is another matter. The Army isn't telling its secrets yet, from all appearances when this was written. Maybe it's a fluke and maybe it isn't. Anyone's guess is pretty good at the moment.

Maybe the thing is still a hoax, as has been the belief of most folks from the start. But something has been found.

The announcement from Eighth Air Force Headquarters by General Ramey that the flying disc was just the radar reflector from a weather balloon effectively killed the story. Most people—especially those in military-dominated areas like New Mexico—were in awe of the government and eager to accept its words. If the USAAF said it was a radar reflector, then who was to disagree? After all, hadn't some of those men carried us to glorious victory in World War II just two years earlier?

But a lot of people knew the wreckage was not part of any weather balloon, or anything else familiar. Some were civilians, not under military control, who could legally spill the beans and leave the government in a very awkward position. Of the newsmen who had seen and probably handled pieces of wreckage obviously unrelated to balloons, all were employees of radio stations. Thinly veiled telephone threats from Washington, aimed at convincing them their station's FCC licenses were in jeopardy if they ever spoke out, worked as planned. Other threats came from what witnesses recall as the office of New Mexico Senator Dennis Chavez, and former Senator and current Secretary of Agriculture Clinton A. Anderson. While similar extralegal behavior on the part of government officials in the 1990s could well produce the opposite result, in 1947 Washington was able to exercise frightening power over a supposedly free, independent press.

Rancher Mac Brazel and his family were neither in the employ of the government nor in need of government approval to work. The technique applied in Mac's case was more direct and at least as illegal: He was taken into custody for about a week, during which time he was persuaded to change his story. It can be assumed that some combination of threats, bribes, and appeals to his patriotism did the trick. He was seen on the streets of Roswell several times during his period of military detention and shocked old friends by completely ignoring them when he passed by.

On July 10 Mac was escorted to the office of the Roswell *Daily Record* by KGFL owner Walt Whitmore and gave the newspaper for publication an interview that bore little similarity to his original story:

Brazel stated that on June 14 he and an 8-year old son, Vernon, were about 7 or 8 miles from the ranch house of the J. B. Foster ranch, which he operates, when they came upon a large area of bright wreckage made up of rubber strips, tinfoil, a rather tough paper and sticks.

At the time Brazel was in a hurry to get his round made and he did not pay much attention to it. But he did remark about what he had seen and on July 4 he, his wife, Vernon and a daughter Betty, age 14, went back to the spot and gathered up quite a bit of the debris.

The next day he first heard about the flying disks, and he wondered if what he had found might be the remnants of one of these.

Monday he came to town to sell some wool and while here he went to see sheriff George Wilcox and "whispered kinda confidential like" that he might have found a flying disc.

Wilcox got in touch with the Roswell Army Air Field and Maj. Jesse A. Marcel and a man in plain clothes accompanied him home, where they picked up the rest of the pieces of the "disc" and went to his home to try to reconstruct it.

According to Brazel they simply could not reconstruct it at all. They tried to make a kite out if it, but could not do that and could not find any way to put it back together so that it would fit.

Then Major Marcel brought it to Roswell and that was the last he heard of it until the story broke that he had found a flying disk.

Brazel said that he did not see it fall from the sky and did not see it before it was torn up, so he did not know the size or shape it might have been, but he thought it might have been about as large as a table top. The balloon which held it up, if that was how it worked, must have been about 12 feet long, he felt, measuring the distance by the size of the room in which he sat. The rubber was smoky gray in color and scattered over an area about 200 yards in diameter.

When the debris was gathered up the tinfoil, paper, tape, and sticks made a bundle about three feet long and 7 or 8 inches thick, while the rubber made a bundle about 18 or 20 inches long and about 8 inches thick. In all, he estimated, the entire lot would have weighed maybe five pounds.

There was no sign of any metal in the area which might have been used for an engine and no sign of any propellers of any kind, although at least one paper fin had been glued onto some of the tinfoil.

There were no words to be found anywhere on the instrument, although there were letters on some of the parts. Considerable Scotch tape and some tape with flowers printed upon it had been used in the construction.

No strings or wires were to be found but there were some eyelets in the paper to indicate that some sort of attachment may have been used.

Brazel said that he had previously found two weather observation balloons on the ranch, *but that what he found this time did not in any way resemble any of these* [emphasis added].

"I am sure what I found was not any weather observation balloon," he said. "But if I find anything else beside a bomb they are going to have a hard time getting me to say anything about it."

Firsthand witnesses agree that Brazel seemed "not himself" at the newspaper and when being escorted around town by military people. But even if he had been, his words should have raised a lot of eyebrows around Roswell, though they were given no exposure elsewhere.

Mac makes clear that he was familiar with weather balloons and that what he found was *not* a weather balloon! He saw the wreckage on the ranch, while General Ramey and company did not. Who was better qualified to describe and identify it? Brazel also said there were no words on it, even though weather balloons are well marked with the owner's name and address so they can be returned for a small reward. But he did say there were letters on some of the parts, which obviously could not be fitted together to form any words.

Weighing heavily against the scattered wreckage being any sort of balloon was its condition: Pieces were spread out over an area of more than 250,000 square feet ("200 yards in diameter"). A helium-filled balloon cannot explode, nor can it hit the ground in such a way that it will be shattered into a lot of pieces. And even if it had, there would hardly have been enough of it to attract attention when spread out over an area the size of several football fields.

And if that isn't enough to make it obvious that what Brazel found was not related to the balloon he described, recall that he said there was "a large area of bright wreckage made up of rubber strips, tinfoil, a rather tough paper and sticks." Tinfoil certainly can be bright and eye-catching, but the same cannot be said for smokey gray rubber, tough paper, and sticks. And if he could bundle all of it up in a couple of small packages, why did the two vehicles of Marcel and Cavitt hold but a small portion of the total they found? Much of the rest of the story told by Mac Brazel on July 10 was totally at odds with what he said before and what has subsequently been well checked out: dates, places, and of course the description of the various types of debris.

While no proof has been found that the government bribed Brazel to change his story and then keep quiet, there is evidence pointing in that direction. In the words of Loretta Proctor, nearest neighbor to the ranch:

"I think that within that year, he had moved off the ranch and moved to Alamagordo or to Tularosa and he put in a locker there. That was before people had home freezers, and it was a large refrigerated building . . . you would buy beef and cut it up and put it in those lockers and you had a key to it and you could get your beef out when you wanted it. I think it would have been pretty expensive, and we kind of wondered how he could put it in with rancher's wages."

Did Mac Brazel see alien bodies in the aftermath of the crash near Corona? He certainly never claimed to have seen bodies, but circumstantial evidence suggests he probably saw at least one, as well as a lot of wreckage.

Had Mac seen nothing more than the sort of scrap material recovered from the sheep ranch by Major Marcel and CICman Cavitt (when accompanied by Brazel), there would hardly have been any need for the army to take such extreme action against him. Why take him into custody for a week and then possibly bribe him to keep quiet about matters which do not seem that serious? He was already on record as having seen a large quantity of scrap material and, while escorted by soldiers, gave a newspaper interview in which he stated clearly that the wreckage was not that of a weather balloon.

Why did the army give him such special treatment if all he knew was common knowledge already? That little cat was out of the bag, leaving no obvious reason for the army to exert unusual pressure on Mac to change his behavior.

It seems entirely possible that he could have been flown over the ranch, which stretched for miles, on a reconnaissance mission, as he knew the land far better than the army did. He could thus have been involved in the discovery of the main part of the craft, which is rumored to have landed some two and a half miles from the field of debris. Had he been in a small plane, such as one of the army's four-passenger Stinson L-5 liaison planes capable of operating off rough ground, he could have seen the disc on the ground.

If the information given civilian mortician Glenn Dennis by the Roswell AAF mortuary officer (see Chapter 9)—that the bodies were found a mile or two from the crashed craft—is correct, their discovery from the air makes sense. Moreover, if what the nurse told Dennis is accurate (that the bodies were found in small "escape capsules" such as he saw in the rear of some GI ambulances) they probably could not have been recognized for what they were from the air. Only from close-up ground observation, after a spotter plane had first seen them and then landed close by.

Brazel, a quiet, rugged cowboy of the old school, died in 1965 before the world had a clue that he had been privy to the most exciting secret of all time. According to his son, Bill Jr., Mac never felt like he had done anything special. He rode out, found a lot of odd-looking stuff and eventually told the government. In the words of the son:

> My Dad found this thing and he told me a little bit about it . . . not much . . . because the Air Force asked him to take an oath that he wouldn't tell anybody in detail about it. He went to his grave and he never told anybody.
>
> He was an oldtime Western cowboy, and they didn't do a lot of talkin'. My brother and I had just went through World War II (him in the Army and me in the Navy) and needless to say, my Dad was proud. Like he told me, "When you guys went in the service, you took an oath, and I took an oath not to tell." The only thing he said was, 'Well, there's a big bunch of stuff, there's some tinfoil, some wood, and on some of that wood there was Japanese or Chinese figures."

Had that been all Mac saw, there would certainly have been no need for the army to make him take an oath not to talk. Not to talk about things that were already public! Clearly, more was involved, and that could have been bodies.

Bill Jr. was living and working in Albuquerque, more than seventy-five miles to the northwest of the ranch, but returned when he realized his father had been taken into custody by the army and thus there was no one to run the ranch:

> I rode out there [the field where the debris was found] on the average of once a week, and I was riding through that area, I was lookin'. That's why I found those little pieces.
>
> Not over a dozen pieces—I'd say maybe eight different pieces—but there was only three [different] items involved: somethin' on the order of balsa wood, something on the order of heavy-gauge monofilament fishing line, and a little piece of—it wasn't tinfoil, it wasn't lead foil—a piece about the size of my finger. Some of it was like balsa wood: real light and kind of neutral color, more of a tan. To the best of my memory, there

wasn't any grain in it. Couldn't break it—it'd flex a little. I couldn't whittle it with my pocket knife.

The "string," I couldn't break it. The only reason I noticed the tinfoil (I'm gonna call it tinfoil), I picked this stuff up and put it in my chaps pocket. Might be two or three days or a week before I took it out and put it in a cigar box. I happened to notice when I put that piece of foil in that box, and the damn thing just started unfolding and just flattened out! Then I got to playin' with it. I'd fold it, crease it, lay it down and it'd unfold. It's kinda weird. I couldn't tear it. The color was in between tinfoil and lead foil, about the [thickness] of lead foil.

I was in Corona, in the bar, the pool hall—sort of the meeting place—domino parlor. . . . That's where everybody got together. Everybody was askin' . . . they'd seen the papers (this was about a month after the crash) and I said, "Oh, I picked up a few little bits and pieces and fragments." So, what are they? "I dunno."

Then, lo and behold, here comes the military (out to the ranch, a day or two later). I'm almost positive that the officer in charge, his name was Armstrong, a real nice guy. He had a [black] sergeant with him that was real nice. I think there was two other enlisted men. They said, "We understand your father found this weather balloon." I said, "Well, yeah!" "And we understand you found some bits and pieces." I said, "Yeah, I've got a cigar box that's got a few of 'em in there, down at the saddle shed."

And this (I think he was a captain), and he said, "Well, we would like to take it with us." I said, "Well. . . ." And he smiled and he said, "Your father turned the rest of it over to us, and you know he's under an oath not to tell. Well," he said, "we came after those bits and pieces." And I kind of smiled and said, "OK, you can have the stuff, I have no use for it at all."

He said, "Well, have you examined it?" And I said, "Well, enough to know that I don't know what the hell it is!" And he said, "We would rather you didn't talk very much about it."

Once again, the military's behavior contradicted its claims that nothing of consequence happened at the sheep ranch. Once again, the military's preoccupation with security succeeded in attracting attention to something that might otherwise have gone unnoticed.

Bill Brazel Jr.'s memory of his limited personal involvement in the Corona crash is clear and sharp. Though he appears, sitting quietly in his simple home, to be a man uninterested in the world beyond the scenic, sparsely populated land of his origins, his duties in the navy and later with a geophysical exploration firm took him around the world twice. His days of travel and adventure may be behind him, but his awareness of the world remains. As does his puzzlement at the behavior of the army so many years ago.

He saw only a few small pieces of the debris that fell on the Foster ranch, yet the attitude of the military when it came to retrieve it convinced him that what fell there was no weather balloon.

A former neighbor of Brazel, Marian Strickland, recalled in 1990 a visit Mac paid to her and her family a week or two after he had been released by the military from his period of confinement. Mac, her late husband Lyman, and several of their children were sitting around the dinner table while she was "carryin' the coffee. I heard pieces of the conversation: How nasty the officers at the air base were. The whole neighborhood was scandalized that the army would treat people like that . . . people who had good intentions.

"He made it plain he was not supposed to tell that there was any excitement about the material (he found on the ranch). He was a man who had integrity. He definitely felt insulted and mis-used, and disrespected. He was worse than annoyed! He was definitely under some stress, and felt that he had been kicked around.

"He was threatened that if he opened his mouth, he might get thrown in the back side of the jail. He gave that impression, definitely."

All this because a ranch foreman saw some shapeless pieces of scrap material? In all probability, there was more to it. While no direct testimony exists that Mac saw bodies, the behavior of the military points in that direction.

*   *   *

At about the same time something eerie happened on the ranch southeast of Corona, something even stranger happened 150 miles to the west. Of the ten or twelve civilians who reportedly saw the second crashed UFO before the military arrived, only two have been willing to talk (one of them has since died) and the others are still being sought. Supporting evidence consists of memories that something very unusual happened there: numerous recollections, but few containing specifics.

The first clue that anything at all had occurred in western New Mexico came from Vern Maltais, whose close friend, Grady "Barney" Barnett, described the amazing scene to him. It was Maltais and his wife Jean who first told Stanton Friedman about this after a lecture in Bemidji, Minnesota, in 1978. According to Maltais, Barnett was working in western New Mexico as a field engineer for the U.S. Soil Conservation Service when he came upon a "large metallic object" stuck in the ground and a group of archaeologists looking at it.

As Vern Maltais recalls, Barnett "noticed they were standing around looking at some dead bodies that had fallen to the ground, I think there were others in the machine, which was a kind of metallic instrument of some sort—a kind of disc. It seemed to be made of stainless steel. The machine had been split open by explosion or impact.

"They were like humans, but they were not humans. The heads were round, the eyes were small, and they had no hair. The eyes were oddly spaced. They were quite small by our standards and their heads were larger in proportion to their bodies than ours. Their clothing seemed to be one piece, and gray in color. You couldn't see any zippers, belts or buttons. They seemed to be all males and there were a number of them."

This, of course, is no more than Vern Maltais' recollection of what Barney Barnett had told him several years before. These are not Barnett's actual words, as he died in 1969 before anyone in the private UFO community had become aware of his involvement in the New Mexico crashes, before anyone had heard of a crash in western New Mexico, and before anyone was taking stories of crashes seriously.

It has been suggested, in the book *The Roswell Incident* and subsequently in *UFO Crash at Roswell* that Barnett stumbled upon the main part of the craft that had left its pieces on the Foster ranch near Corona, rather than another craft that had crashed well to the west. In the absence of direct testimony from Barnett, all one has is secondhand information, but it all points away from Corona.

James Fleck Danley, Barney's boss, has made it clear that Barney's territory extended to the west of his office in Socorro, not to the north or east. A diary kept by Barney's wife and provided by her niece, Alice Knight, shows that his field trips were to the west, the "high country," to towns like Datil and Magdalena and to ranches in the area of the Plains of San Augustin. All of this is to the west, away from Corona.

A former neighbor, Harold Baca, responding to a letter in the Socorro newspaper from Stanton Friedman seeking people who had known Barney, said Barney told him about the flying saucer that had crashed "out in the Plains." An oldtime rancher on the Plains, the late Marvin Ake, told Stanton Friedman that he had heard of a crashed saucer story "out on the Plains." A retired postmistress from Datil told Friedman of a crashed saucer "out on the Plains" that had been brought out through Magdalena at night.

As additional support for the contention that Barnett had indeed encountered a crashed saucer and alien bodies is the testimony of William Leed, a career military officer. In a recent conversation, Leed told Friedman that in the early 1960s he was advised by a colonel familiar with his interest in UFOs to talk to a man who had touched one: "Barney Barnett." Leed, when in the Southwest, made a special side trip to see Barnett. Although Leed was there as a private citizen, Barnett asked for his military credentials. Leed was then told of Barney's walking up to the crashed craft and seeing alien bodies, and of his interrogation by military people on at least three occasions, and the strong suggestion that he not talk about his experience. Leed said he had no reason to think Barnett was telling him anything but the truth.

Despite heroic efforts to find additional witnesses, little more was learned about the San Agustin crash for a decade. Then, in response to the immensely popular January 1990 *Unsolved Mysteries* telecast about the Corona crash, a man named Gerald Anderson called the producer to announce he had more information that might be of interest. The message was passed along to both Kevin Randle and Stanton Friedman, who had worked on the show and who were busily trying to chase down other leads to the crash stories. A personality conflict between Anderson and Randle cut that relationship short, but the new witness hit it off much better with Friedman, who taped a long telephone interview and began a long and complicated series of maneuvers aimed at getting a copy of a personal journal allegedly kept by Anderson's late Uncle Ted. In late 1990, Anderson and the authors traveled to the Plains of San Agustin to see if Jerry could relive his experiences of forty-three years earlier.

Brought to the area by helicopter, Jerry jumped out as soon as it touched down and raced to what he thought was the very place he had seen the wrecked craft and its crew of small humanoids. His undisguised excitement created an atmosphere of authenticity, as he later led the others to significant locations, pointing, gesturing, and exclaiming as he went. Everything suggested that he had finally returned to the place where something traumatic had happened to a six-year-old who now, standing six-four and carrying a muscular 250-plus pounds, resembled an offensive guard.

The Plains of San Agustin is a vast level area in western New Mexico that was once a great lake providing water for prehistoric tribes, and more recently their ancient artifacts for archeologists. On the southeast side is Bat Cave, famous as the site of the discovery of kernels of corn said to be at least forty-five hundred years old and the remnants of the earliest known agriculture in North America. The Plains are about seven thousand feet above sea level and are surrounded by peaks of the Tularosa, Black, and Datil Mountains reaching up to ninety-five hundred feet. The air is dry and thin.

At the northern end of the Plains (locally called the Playa)
stands a group of twenty-seven large (eighty-two-foot-
diameter) steerable radio telescopes called the Very Large Array; stretching as much as thirteen miles along each arm of a Y,
it is the largest radiotelescope in the world. But in 1947, there
were no radio telescopes. Just mountains, crude roads, the occasional rustic ranchhouse, the flatness of the plains, and the
rocky peaks. The Continental Divide, spine of the Rocky
Mountains, runs just to the west. And less than a hundred
miles to the east sits Trinity Site, where the world's first
atomic bomb was tested in 1945. The Plains are sixty miles
long and ten to fifteen miles wide, steeped in traditions both
old and new.

It was to this area, with the intention of hunting a type of
rock called moss agate, that young Gerald Anderson came with
his older brother Glenn, his uncle Ted, his father, and his
cousin Victor on a very hot, humid morning in early July 1947.
Jerry and his immediate family had just moved to Albuquerque
a few days before, and several of them had driven south with
other relatives who had lived there much longer. At midmorn-
ing, the group of men and boys parked their car after driving as
far off the two-lane road as the terrain would permit.

They proceeded along a dried-out river bed called an arroyo,
the boys bounding over the rough ground, eager for adventure
despite the oppressive heat. They got to the end of a small
stand of trees which had blocked their view to the west and
their world changed forever. As Jerry described it to the authors
more than forty years later:

"We came around the bend in the arroyo, and Victor said, "Hey,
look at that, there's something over there!" We were two to three
hundred feet away. What we saw was a silver object, a circular
silver object stuck in the ground, kind of at an angle. It was
jammed into a hillside. Seemed to me there was more than one
tree that had been knocked down. It was kinda balanced up on
one of the trees.
Initially, I really didn't realize what everybody was hollering

about. And then when they said "Crash!," and then when I finally saw it, when I realized what I was looking at . . . then it crossed my mind that it was a dirigible, a blimp that had crashed. I don't know why, I think it was one airship I was familiar with, because back in that era they were quite large and quite awesome. I kinda had a "thing" about blimps.

We headed straight toward it, and there was one point when we got up close to it, my Dad told me to stay back. Fifty to sixty feet: we were practically on top of it. There was a big gouge mark where it had cut a big furrow across the arroyo from another hill on the other side. It tore up a lot of the sagebrush and there was small fires smoldering here and there.

That's when my brother said, "That's a goddamn spaceship! Them's Martians!"

Then everyone was runnin' around in circles. I didn't stay put—I think I was scared—I went over there with 'em. And there were three of these crewmembers laid out on the ground, under the edge of this thing, in a shaded area, and there was one sitting upright. The ones that were laying on the ground, two of 'em weren't moving at all, they were just laying there.

They looked like they had some sort of bandages on 'em. One of them had it over his arm. The one that I touched had it around his midsection and partially over his shoulder. It appeared to be, as I think back on it now, the one that was still alive and moving had given first aid to the others. And the one next to him was breathing very erratically and its chest was heaving in an unnatural way. He was obviously in distress . . . very badly so.

The other two didn't move at all. The only one that really moved was the one that was sitting up, and it obviously was scared to death of us. It was scooting backward against the underside of the saucer. It was obviously terrified of us.

At first [the adults] just kind of oohed and ahhed around. My cousin Victor, as usual, was into everything, in everybody's way. My brother, Glenn, was looking over the saucer-shaped object. He pulled Victor off it; Victor was up on the rim where the gash was, and he grabbed him by his legs and pulled him off and told him to stay out of there because he could cause it to explode.

And Glenn went on up there and was hanging half-in, half-out of that gash in the side, and I was standing there watching him.

And while I was doing this, Dad and Ted were kneeling down next to this creature that was alive, and Ted was trying to talk to it in Spanish and it wasn't responding. When someone moved suddenly, it would recoil and put its hands up like it was afraid it was going to be hit.

It seemed to be in pretty good shape. Its uniform was torn in a couple spots. The others, they were obviously injured, their uniforms were in pretty sad shape. They looked like they'd been through a helluva fight! I didn't see anything that looked like blood, though. There was some kind of a container, a metal box, next to this one that was alive, that had this same kind of [bandagelike] material in it and some other stuff in it. It may have been a first-aid kit.

The one [whose] chest was moving funny, one leg didn't quite look right, like it might have had a fracture. The others really didn't show any deformities or anything like that. I'm convinced that the one I [touched], his eyes was open, staring blankly, was dead. It felt dead when I touched it, it was very cold. In looking back now, I think it was probably rigor mortis, 'cause it was stiffened up by this time. The odd part about it is, I've often wondered why the other one didn't cover him up. We cover up dead humans because I think we're afraid to look at dead things. I think it's funny it didn't cover up its dead crew members like that. Unless that doesn't mean anything to 'em.

See, I thought they were dolls. I didn't think they were real, even though I'd seen this one moving and reacting.

I remember putting my hand against the side of the saucer, and it was cold, almost like it was refrigerated. Being out there in the sun and being real shiny, I probably expected it to be hot, but it wasn't. It was very cold! Like it was wintertime and you were touching something metal. And the area right next to it was very cool, compared to the other areas around [there]. The area around the spaceship was blazing hot. I remember the desert sun: It was unbelievably hot.

How close did he get to the alien that was alive?

I was about as close as you are to me right now—we're what, about three feet apart? I didn't get as close as my Dad and my uncle, 'cause they were kneeling, squatting down right next to it. At one point, my uncle Ted had reached out and touched it on the shoulder like he was trying to console it. At that point it wasn't recoiling in fear anymore. I was very close to him when he did this . . . about three feet away.

Was it aware of your presence?

It looked around at all of us. It was like it was trying to watch everybody at once. I think that might be one of the reasons that I picked up on it being afraid. It acted like a cat that was around kids. It just constantly watched everybody. It looked at me several times. It seemed very uneasy, even when it had calmed down to a certain degree.

Why did you go around behind the craft?

Because Glenn was around there . . . I went around to see where my brother was. My brother was up on the edge of this thing and he was looking inside that rip in the side. He cut himself on the side of his face, or nicked himself. And I went around to that side when he came out and I could see in there where he was at, because the saucer was tilted, the edge was tilted down and jammed in at that point. I could see directly into it, and was looking through the outer hull and into another bulkhead, and that bulkhead was shaped exactly like the outer hull.

You could see through the rip, and you could see what looked like components (I don't know if they were electrical, electronic, propulsion, or what). They were all seemingly hooked together by these cables—clusters of threadlike material in the form of a cable—and one of these was hanging out of that rip. There were several hundred strands per one of these clusters, they were wrapped. They blew in the wind like a horse's tail, except there was lights all over the ends of them. These lights were undulating, they were flashing. Some of them were bright, some of them were very dim, some of them were flashing. They looked like fire on the ends of these threadlike things that were waving in the breeze.

And you could see others of those went from one kind of

package of components to another kind of package, kind of like they were cables of some kind. And down the center between these things—they were all in very neat little rows—there was, like, scribbling. [On] each one of these component boxes there would be scribbling, it was almost a pink color on sort of a brown, woodlike background. Like it was writing or symbols that explained what this thing was.

You could see some other lights in there. These lights were usually associated with components. Some of them were going on and off. The light would go off over here, and the light over here would come on. It was like circuitry was still functioning, or attempting to function. There was some [that were] amber, and some green.

Were they the same color as the lights on the threads that were hanging down?

Some of that was really brilliant red, and some of it was like brilliant white. Strobe-light bright. The others were red, they were incredibly brilliant colors and they were fading. Some of them would fade, they were very faint, and others were brilliant and real obvious. Some of them appeared to be fluctuating in intensity . . . getting real bright, and then dim, and then partially bright, and then real bright, and then dim again.

I never got up in that crack. Glenn [said] that it was very cold. I knew that, as I'd already touched that portion of the outer hull.

How big was the gash?

Eight to ten feet from bottom to top. It went almost from the edge of the saucer to the top of the dome. And probably in width: three feet. It was an elliptically shaped vertical gash, like a parenthesis. The widest part of it seemed to be toward the center. It looked like it had been pulled open and all the metal turned in, and it was very ripped and jagged.

There was a real strong smell, too. Like, maybe, rubbing alcohol or acetone or something like that. And this is what I think was prompting my Dad to jump on my brother's back constantly about his cigarettes, because he was afraid he was gonna blow the place up!

Right after that, these people came up the arroyo toward us from the opposite direction from where we had come. There was a man and five of his students—three guys and two girls—college-age students. They were in their late teens and twenties.

The newcomers included five college students and their professor, Dr. Buskirk. They had been working on an archaeological dig near cliff dwellings a few miles away and had decided to hike over after seeing what they thought was a fiery meteor crashing the night before. When they arrived their reactions closely paralleled those of Jerry and his relatives:

First with: "I don't believe what I'm seeing!," and then with shock when they realized these weren't dolls, that these were live, but nobody knew what they were. And here's this funny craft, and Glenn and them was still talking about men from Mars and stuff like this.

Dr. Buskirk apparently is capable of speaking several languages, because he had tried to communicate with this creature. He knelt down there with Ted and my Dad and tried to talk to this thing. I recognized one of the languages as German because I had German relatives that spoke German fluently. Ted was married to a Mexican woman and he spoke Spanish, so I understood that one. Of course, they got no response. I recall this Dr. Buskirk tried sign language, and there was apparently no response from that.

And then another guy just showed up suddenly. I had went up the bank and was standing there by the trees, right by the saucer on top of the rocks. And there was a guy with a pick-up [truck], and it was one of those old-model pick-ups and it had a whip antenna on it, like a police car has. He walked over there and he looked like Harry Truman: he had a real ruddy complexion, he wore glasses and he had sort of khaki work clothes on and he had a straw hat. Back in those days, even the little kids knew who Harry Truman was: He beat the Germans and the Japs!

This guy looked like him, and he walked over there and he got to talkin' to Dr. Buskirk and Ted and my brother and my Dad, and he said that he had seen it from out on the Playa. He had apparently worked out there, and he acknowledged that he made maps or something like that. [It is assumed that this man was Barney Barnett.]

At this point, with almost a dozen people swarming around the wrecked craft and the four strange little beings, the U.S. Army arrived and everything changed.

The bulk of the detail on the San Agustin crash comes from one man who had been just a youngster at the time of the incident. Charges have been made that Gerald Anderson invented the story of seeing wreckage and bodies. In 1991 the Fund for UFO Research paid for a polygraph examination of Anderson. The American Polygraph Association was contacted and recommended a member in the area, a man named Robert Riggs—a professional polygraph examiner for over ten years and himself a former policeman.

Riggs first met alone with Friedman for over an hour to review the story and a whole host of possible hoax scenarios. He then met with Anderson for more than two hours checking on all aspects of the story. Finally, he hooked Gerald up to the machine and asked his key questions. At the end of this session Riggs informed Friedman that he found no evidence of deception or of pathology, and that Anderson had an outstanding memory.

While no other firsthand witnesses have been found to corroborate Anderson's testimony, Friedman did find a member of his father's church who recalled overhearing the father talking to two men about a flying disc and government people restricting his access to it. (This conversation took place after Gerald's father had retired from his job at Sandia Corporation, where he had required a high-level security clearance because of the company's nuclear weapons–related manufacturing activities.)

Psychiatric social worker John Carpenter, who trained at the Menninger Clinic, has worked with Gerald for more than a year. They have gone over and over the complicated story, at times using regressive hypnosis in an effort to bring out greater detail and to search for any significant inconsistencies. Carpenter is highly impressed by Anderson and is convinced he is telling the truth as he knows it. Carpenter sees no basis for challenging Anderson's honesty or motives. And Jerry's story is backed up by a journal said to have been written by his Uncle Ted. A copy of this journal was sent directly to Stanton Friedman by Jerry's cousin, now a Catholic nun, accompanied by the following note:

> With this mailing I want no more involvement in this sorry scenario, nor does my mother. Both Maria and I have been transferred to another convent and our Mother has been moved. This family has been plagued by this incident for years and it is far beyond time that such should stop. Why Gerald would wish to reopen this is completely beyond me, I suppose he has his reasons. My father was obsessed with this unearthly horror and kept several journals to prevent others from getting to them. Wreckage and debris from the crash, along with a larger journal are buried out there. . . .
>
> I pray each and every day that God will grant protection not only to Gerald, but all of you who are involved in this. If these can help you in your quest, then so be it, but you must at this point honor [my] desire to no longer be involved.

Forensic examination of the journal revealed that it was written no earlier than about 1970, but Gerald Anderson had already explained that Glenn had made several copies. So far, attempts to locate the bits of wreckage and the larger journal have proved unsuccessful.

Once the army arrived at both crash sites, civilian involvement became severely restricted.

8

The Military Takes Over

A T BOTH primary New Mexico crash sites, civilians were on the scene well in advance of anyone from the government. Had they not seen enough to convince themselves that something extremely unusual had happened, it is doubtful that anyone would ever have heard this story. Luck, in the form of those who were on the spot for other reasons, thus played a vital role in one of history's great stories.

A large quantity of debris from a "flying saucer" lay in a field outside Corona, New Mexico, for several days before anyone connected with the U.S. government had a clue that it was there. Apparently it was deposited on the sheep ranch on the night of Wednesday, July 2, and was found the next morning by Foster Ranch foreman William "Mac" Brazel when he rode out to check on possible damage to fences or windmills from the previous evening's severe electrical storm.

The government's first indication of a strange occurrence came a little after noon on Sunday, July 6, when Brazel paid a visit to Chaves County Sheriff George Wilcox to show him a few samples of the odd material he had found. Wilcox looked it over and was sufficiently impressed to call the Roswell Army Air Field intelligence officer, Maj. Jesse Marcel. Marcel drove the short distance to the sheriff's office, inspected the scraps, and was thoroughly puzzled by their unique appearance. He reported this to his commanding officer, Col. William "Butch" Blanchard, telling him of the field full of debris and of the odd characteristics of the pieces he had just seen.

Blanchard reacted quickly, ordering Major Marcel to get someone from the Counter-Intelligence Corps office and proceed to the ranch with Brazel. They were ordered to collect as much of the material as they could load into their two vehicles and bring it back to the airbase.

Soon after this, military police converged on the sheriff's office, took possession of the scraps Brazel had left there, and delivered them to Blanchard's office. Testimony from several enlisted men points to the material then being flown to Eighth Air Force headquarters in Fort Worth, Tex., and from there to Washington, per specific instructions. Someone had obviously informed Washington that something important was going on in New Mexico.

Meanwhile, Marcel and CIC captain Cavitt arrived at the Foster ranch late Sunday night, having struggled over terrible roads and some stretches where they had to drive cross-country. They spent the night in sleeping bags in a small building and in the morning were taken by Mac Brazel to the place he had found the material. In 1979, Jesse Marcel described his experience:

> When we arrived at the crash site, it was amazing to see the vast amount of area it covered. It was nothing that hit the ground or exploded [on] the ground. It's something that must have exploded above ground, traveling perhaps at a high rate of speed ... we don't know. But it scattered over an area of about three quarters of a mile long, I would say, and fairly wide, several hundred feet wide. So we proceeded to pick up all the fragments we could find and load up our Jeep Carry-All. It was quite obvious to me, [from my] familiar[ity] with air activities, that it was not a weather balloon, nor was it an airplane or a missile. What was it, we didn't know. We just picked up the fragments. It was something I had never seen before, and I was pretty familiar with all air

activities. We loaded up the Carry-All but I wasn't satisfied. I told Cavitt, "You drive this vehicle back to the base and I'll go back out there and pick up as much as I can put in the car," which I did. But we picked up only a very small portion of the material that was there.

One thing that impressed me about the debris that we were referring to is the fact that a lot of it looked like parchment. A lot of it had a lot of little members [I beams] with symbols that we had to call them hieroglyphics because I could not interpret them, they could not be read; they were just symbols, something that meant something and they were not all the same. The members that this was painted on—by the way, those symbols were pink and purple . . . uh . . . lavender was actually what it was. And . . . uh . . . so these little members could not be broken, could not be burned . . . I even tried to burn that. It would not burn. The same with the parchment we had.

But something that is more astounding is that the piece of metal that we brought back was so thin, just like the tinfoil in a pack of cigarette paper. I didn't pay too much attention to that at first, until one of the GIs came to me and said, "You know the metal that was in there? I tried to bend that stuff and it won't bend. I even tried it with a sledge hammer. You can't make a dent on it."

I didn't go back to look at it, myself, again, because we were busy in the office and I had quite a bit of work to do. I am quite sure that this young fellow would not have lied to me about that, because he was a very truthful, very honest guy, so I accepted his word for that. So, beyond that, I didn't actually see him hit the matter with a sledge hammer, but he said, "It's definite that it cannot be bent and it's so light that it doesn't weigh anything." And that was true of all the material that was brought up. It was so light that it weighed practically nothing.

This particular piece of metal was, I would say, about two feet long and perhaps a foot wide. See, that stuff weighs nothing, it's so thin, it isn't any thicker than the tinfoil in a pack of cigarettes. So, I tried to bend the stuff [but] it wouldn't bend. We even tried making a dent in it with a sixteen-pound sledge hammer. And there was still no dent in it. I didn't have the time to go out there and find out more about it, because I had so much other work to do that I just let it go. It's still a mystery to me as to what the whole thing was. Like I said before, I knew quite a bit about the material used in the air, but it was nothing I had seen before. And as of now, I still don't know what it was. So that's how it stands.

Once high-ranking (and thus influential) people in the military realized they were dealing with very unusual materials beyond their experience, they quickly organized a mission to recover all of it, in order to learn as much about it as they could and to make certain it did not fall into the wrong (meaning public) hands. Whatever it was, it had to be kept secret at least until the top brass in Fort Worth or Washington could decide what to do with it.

A large group of soldiers was sent to the "debris field" on the sheep ranch near Corona, including a lot of MPs whose job it was to limit access to those the army wanted on the scene. It was apparent that the scraps in the field were not all of whatever-it-had-been, and so a wide search was launched to find the rest. This was undoubtedly done on the ground (using Jeeps and trucks) and from the air, probably using small liaison planes suitable for rough-field landings if necessary.

It couldn't have been more than a day or two before the expanded search paid off. A few miles from the debris field the main body of the craft was located, and a mile or two from that several bodies of small humanoids were found. The startling news (possibly including the word that one of the humanoids was still alive) was shot back to headquarters, and the entire nature of the operation changed. Any lingering thoughts that the debris could have come from some advanced Soviet missile or aircraft vanished with the realization that the crew, and therefore the craft, were not from the Earth!

An important operation instantly became an absolutely vital mission. Never before in history had anything like this happened: Man had just come face to face with beings from another world. Decades of Buck Rogers and Flash Gordon and B movies paled by comparison with this startling reality. We were being visited by an advanced civilization whose motives were totally unknown. Were they friendly scientific explorers, or were they an advance party paving the way for an invasion? If their motives were warlike, did we stand any chance against those who could build craft capable of carrying them untold millions of miles? What would happen, say, if their friends came looking for them?

While Major (later Lieutenant Colonel) Marcel talked about his experiences in the late 1970s, Sheridan Cavitt has refused even to acknowledge that he was there at the ranch with Marcel. However, another Counterintelligence Corps man from Roswell, Bill Rickett, has recently spoken out on his experiences a few days after the start of official involvement:

"[The material] was very strong and very light. You could bend it but couldn't crease it. As far as I know, no one ever figured out what it was made of."

Rickett escorted Dr. Lincoln LaPaz, famed meteor expert from the New Mexico Institute of Meteoritics, on a tour of the crash site and surrounding area.

It was LaPaz's job to try to find out what the speed and trajectory of the thing was. LaPaz was a world-renowned expert on trajectories of objects in the sky, especially meteors, and I was told to give him all the help I could.

At one point LaPaz interviewed the farmer [Mac Brazel]. I remember something coming up during their conversation about this fellow thinking that some of his animals had acted strangely after this thing happened. Dr. LaPaz seemed very interested in this for some reason.

LaPaz wanted to fly over the area, and this was arranged. He found one other spot where he felt this thing had touched down and then taken off again. The sand at this spot had been turned into a glasslike substance. We collected a boxful of samples of this material—as I recall, there were some metal samples here, too, of that same sort of thin foil stuff. LaPaz sent this box off somewhere for study; I don't know or recall where, but I never saw it again. This place was some miles from the other one.

LaPaz was very good at talking to people, especially some of the local ranch hands who didn't speak a lot of English. LaPaz spoke Spanish. I remember he found a couple of people who had

seen two—I don't know what to call them; UFOs, I suppose—
anyway, had seen two of these things fly over very slowly at a
very low altitude on a date, in the evening, that he determined
had been a day or two after the other one had blown up. These
people said something about animals being affected, too. . . .

Before he went back to Albuquerque, he told me that he was
certain that this thing had gotten into trouble, that it had
touched down for repairs, taken off again, and then exploded. He
also felt certain there were more than one of these devices, and
that the others had been looking for it—at least that's what he
said. He was positive the thing had malfunctioned.

The Air Force's explanation that it was a balloon was totally
untrue. It was not a balloon. I never did know for sure what its
purpose was, but it wasn't ours. I remember speculating with
LaPaz that it might have been some higher civilization checking
on us. LaPaz wasn't against the idea, but said he was going to
leave speculations out of his report.

Dr. LaPaz, who had been deeply involved in a 1950s study of
"green fireballs" that had some UFO characteristics, unfortunately died before anyone became aware of his involvement
in the New Mexico crash episode. His report is one of the many
documents the government has been able to conceal from the
public for more than forty years.

In general, the government has done a wonderful job of keeping all details of the crashes secret. Few names of military
people and others who visited the sites are known, and those
who are known have, in most cases, been unwilling to talk.
With one fascinating exception. In November 1990 Stanton
Friedman was able to cap months of negotiations by interview-
ing, in person, a man who says in a most believable fashion that
he was there and he saw.

F. B. was an Army Air Forces photographer stationed at Anacostia Naval Air Station, Washington, D.C., when he and fellow photographer A. K. were hustled aboard an army B-25
bomber and flown to Roswell Army Air Field sometime during
the second week of July 1947. He told Friedman:

One morning they came in and they said, "Pack up your bags and
we'll have the cameras there, ready for you." We didn't know

where we was goin'. [His 4x5 Speed Graphic press camera was on
the plane, and after a few hours' flight, they arrived at Roswell.]
We got in a staff car with some of the gear they had brought along
with us in trucks, and we headed out . . . about an hour and a half
. . . we was headin' north.

We got out there [one of the three crash sites in the Corona
area] and there was a helluva lot of people out there, in a closed
tent. You couldn't hardly see anything inside the tent. They said,
"Set your camera up to take a picture fifteen feet away." A. K. got
in a truck and headed out to where they was pickin' up pieces.
All kinds of brass runnin' around. And they was tellin' us what
to do: Shoot this, shoot that! There was an officer in charge. He
met us out there and he'd go into the tent and he'd come back and
tell us, "OK." He'd stand there right besides us and [say], "OK,
take this picture!"

There was four bodies I could see when the flash went off, but
you was almost blind because it was a beautiful day . . . sunny.
You'd go in this tent, which was awful dark. That's all I was
takin': bodies. These bodies was under a canvas, and they'd open
it up and you'd take a picture, flip out your flashbulb, put another
one in [take another picture] and give him the film holder (each
holder held two sheets of four-by-five inch cut film) and then you
went to the next spot.

I guess there was ten to twelve officers, and when I got ready to
go in, they'd all come out. The tent was about twenty by thirty
foot. The bodies looked like they was lyin' on a tarp. One guy did
all the instructions. He'd take a flashlight and he'd come down
there: "See this flashlight?" Yes, sir! "You're in focus with it?"
Yes, sir! "Take a picture of this." He'd take the flashlight away. We
just moved around in a circle, takin' pictures. Seemed to me [the
bodies] were all just about identical. Dark-complected. I remember they was thin, and it looked like they had too big of a head. I
took thirty shots . . . I think I had about fifteen [film] holders. It
smelled funny in there.

A. K. came back in a truck that was loaded down with debris.
A lot of pieces stickin' out that wasn't there when they took off.
We got debriefed on the way back to the airport [Roswell Army
Air Field]. About four the next morning, they woke us, they took
us to the mess hall, we ate, we got back on the B-25 and headed
back. When we got back to Anacostia we got debriefed some

more, by a lieutenant commander. [It was made clear to both
F. B. and his friend A. K. that whatever they *thought* they saw in
New Mexico, they hadn't seen.]

There must have been scores of men who were involved in
one way or another in the recovery of the bodies and wreckage
from the three crash sites in the Corona area: the debris field
first discovered by Mac Brazel, the place where the craft
landed, and the place where the bodies were found in their
"escape capsules" and where, one assumes, F. B. took his photographs. Few of these men have been located, and most can be
presumed to have died long before anyone thought to approach
them for interviews.

In the case of the crash by the Plains of San Agustin, 150
miles to the west, the arrival of the military was observed by
about a dozen civilians: Gerald Anderson and his family, a
group of student archaeologists or geologists, and government
engineer Barney Barnett. Of these, Barnett told several friends
a little about his experience, and Anderson has gone into great
detail about what happened when the army showed up while
he and the others were trying to make some sense out of a
shocking experience.

According to Barnett's good friend Vern Maltais, he said,
"While we were looking at [the bodies], a military officer drove
up on a truck with a driver and took control. He told everybody
that the Army was taking over and to get out of the way. Other
military personnel came up and cordoned off the area. We were
told to leave the area and not to talk to anyone about what we
had seen . . . that it was our patriotic duty to remain silent."

Gerald Anderson, in a September 1990, interview, went into
considerably more detail:

> The first thing that showed up, if I remember correctly, was a car
> that looked like ours. And it came up from behind, and it had
> driven right out to this thing, across the prairie there, the desert
> part. He was parked right over here [the site he and the authors
> had just visited]: There's the saucer, and here's those rocks and
> right here's that flat area that we walked through.

I think the first one was that old military Plymouth, and it had some kind of red flag . . . a pennant like football fans take to the stadium. There was a big star on the side of it, and then there was another vehicle behind, that was a smaller, Jeeplike truck that had a bunch of radios in it and two big antennas. There was a guy sittin' in there wearin' earphones and he was talkin' on the radio. And then behind them was two of these big Army transport trucks with the covered-wagon–type tops. Was full of these soldiers and they [got out] here; they were wearin' khaki uniforms and MP patches, and they had clubs and guns on their hips, and they were all carryin' rifles.

They all came down here, screaming and hollering and running us away from [the saucer]. There was a black soldier drivin' the car, and there was an officer with red hair that got out of the car, and he turned out to be the biggest [bleep] of all times. He was obviously in command, and let everybody know it real quick.

He came down there and they started threatening people and pushing people around. I remember my Uncle Ted smacked one of them and knocked him right on his ass . . . this guy just shoved him with a rifle and Ted just hit him! And then this Dr. Buskirk and my Dad grabbed [Ted] and pulled him back. [The soldiers] was makin' all kinds of threats and everything. They told 'em that they was never gonna see their kids again, that they was gonna go to jail if they ever opened their mouths. They threatened this one student . . . they told him they knew he was a foreigner and they could take care of him real good!

This red-headed guy . . . was a captain (because my brother told me he was a captain) . . . his name was Armstrong, and that was printed on the uniform. They never frisked anybody, [but] they took everybody's name and everything. Then they run us all out of there. They made us go back up north, up the arroyo, toward where we parked our car. They made Dr. Buskirk and the five students go up the arroyo with us . . . all of us in a group. And there were soldiers with us.

[Dr. Buskirk] protested and argued with them constantly that he had to go back the other way, that this was the wrong way for them to go, they had to go back the other way [where their car and equipment were]. But I don't remember seein' the other man, the one everybody suspects might have been Barnett; I don't remember him goin' up that gulley with us.

[The soldiers] were really hateful ... they were hateful to everybody there. When we got back up there to the car, this black sergeant came up there, too. And Dr. Buskirk told him, "We gotta go the other way, that's where we came from. We gotta go and get our stuff. We can't go out this way." And so they took them back down the gulley, and the soldiers made us go back up this way, and then all of a sudden, here's Buskirk and his five students again. That other group of soldiers brought 'em in one of those Jeeplike vehicles.

These soldiers made us go back out, and as we drove out, they walked along with us. We got out to the highway and the place was crawling with soldiers. There was barricades and everything. And the last time we saw Buskirk and the five students, they were standing there and Buskirk was pointing toward the landing site again, and was talking to another soldier that Glenn said looked like another officer. They made us go east on the highway toward Datil. Told us "Don't stop, keep goin', don't come back!"

The last thing I saw as I looked back, and I could see the saucer stuck in the ground, just as we started around them trees, I looked back and there was a lot of soldiers and they were all around that disc, and I couldn't see the crew [of the saucer] that was layin' on the ground anymore. There was some other machinery and stuff that had come down off the side and was pulling up there, stopping. It was one of those trucks that had pulled right up there to the crash site.

Soldiers were moving around. There were a lot of things happening back there. They were stretching out cables of some kind. Looked like they were stretching stuff out on the ground, dragging stuff out of these trucks. There was a lot of 'em just standing around. But there was a frenzy of activity back there. Just as soon as they got us out of there, everything just started getting frenzied back there.

When we got up [to the main road], they already had the fence down and they were bringing stuff through, and I remember there was a Jeep that was pulling a trailer with a motor on it, like a generator. When we got on the road, it was Ted that said, "Can we go back over to the store and get somethin' to drink?" "No!

You go that way (the soldier pointed east) and you go that way now!" It was very hostile, and very direct, and to the point.

Once the Andersons had been chased away from the crash site and were on their way home, the military could proceed as it wished with no one to observe. Material was removed to parts unknown, though White Sands/Alamagordo has been suggested, as have Los Alamos and Sandia Base. These areas had the scientific facilities to make possible some analysis of the wreckage and even bodies, and both were highly secure. But the clues are not what one would hope . . . yet.

Somewhere, there is a very large quantity of material, and probably some quite large pieces of two or more UFOs that came to rest within the borders of the United States and maybe in one or more friendly nations. Exactly where they are is a mystery. Even the pieces that went to Wright Field from Roswell AAF and Fort Worth AAF may not be there today. They could well have been moved many times for reasons of security and scientific research.

Rumors abound that the U.S.A. has been involved in attempting to fly a captured UFO from one of its very secret bases in Nevada. Some individuals have even claimed that we have worked closely with actual aliens to adapt their technology to our uses. And that some of our early "stealth" airplanes—the Lockheed F-117 stealth fighter and the Northrop B-2 stealth bomber, in particular—have benefited from "outside" assistance. Absolutely nothing has been offered to support these extreme claims, and so they must be considered no more than rumors. The authors feel they may even be disinformation planted by unnamed government representatives to further confuse the UFO scene.

On a much more reasonable level, it has been suggested that the first UFO material to be retrieved was so technically advanced that it could not be understood even by our top scientists. The analogy has been made with the hypothetical gift of a modern digital electronic watch to Leonardo da Vinci, one of the true geniuses. Not only would he have been unable to understand how it worked, but he would not have had the slightest clue about how he might try to figure it out. Its postage-stamp-size chip would have meant nothing, nor would its liquid crystal display. He would have had no choice but to set it aside in hopes that someone would learn something in the future to enable the strange little gadget to be figured out.

The same could be true of the UFOs that crashed in New Mexico in 1947: They may have been so far ahead of our science and technology that efforts to understand even small parts of them would have proved utterly futile. They would then have been placed in storage and checked periodically to see if the latest knowledge might have shed some light on their exotic make-up.

We may still be waiting for our knowledge of science to catch up.

Or we may have figured out some of what makes a 1947 model UFO tick and have put this knowledge to use. Or we may actually have learned how an alien craft is built, is operated, and is flown.

9

Retrieval and Shipment

D ETAILS of the retrieval of wreckage and bodies from the
Corona and Plains of San Agustin crash sites are skimpy.
As this was all done by the military in remote areas
where the few residents were consciously patriotic, it was a lot
easier to keep secret the details than elements of the crashes
that had been observed by civilians. Just who was involved, and
where the remains were taken, is still a subject for investigation.

What is known is that Mac Brazel started it all by bringing a
few samples of debris from the Foster ranch to the office of
Sheriff George Wilcox in Roswell on July 6. After Major Marcel
and CICman Cavitt left Roswell for the ranch, the samples
apparently were left behind at the sheriff's office, as there was
no point in taking them back to the ranch. According to the
daughters of Sheriff Wilcox, interviewed in 1990, the army
arrived, created quite a stir, and took the strange pieces away.
They almost certainly went straight to the office of Roswell
Army Air Field commander Col. William Blanchard.

Just what Blanchard did with the samples can only be surmised, but it seems increasingly likely that he had them flown
to Eighth Air Force headquarters in Fort Worth, Texas, where

Eighth Air Force commander Gen. Roger Ramey took control of them. According to retired Brig. Gen. Thomas Jefferson Du-Bose, interviewed in 1990 by Stanton Friedman, material from the Corona crash site was at Fort Worth two or three days before the July 8 press conference at which General Ramey promoted the phony "weather balloon" story.

Those samples could have arrived at Fort Worth while Marcel and Cavitt were still on their way to the Foster ranch, and while hardly anyone else in the world was aware that anything unusual had happened near Corona. This was probably the small amount of material that then-colonel DuBose saw wrapped in plastic and attached to the wrist of Col. Al Clarke, base commander at Fort Worth. With his precious cargo treated like secret diplomatic correspondence, Clarke was flown to Washington, D.C., on the direct orders of Gen. Clemence McMullen, acting commander of the Strategic Air Command at Andrews AAF. It was McMullen who gave the telephone order to DuBose to rush the scraps there by "colonel courier" and to concoct a cover story to mislead the press. What happened to the material when it got to Washington is unknown, but it well could have played a major role in convincing those two thousand miles from the New Mexico desert that something of cosmic significance had happened.

When Marcel and Cavitt returned to Roswell Army Air Field early on the morning of July 8, they brought with them two carloads of debris. It was this, or at least most of it, that Marcel accompanied on a flight to Fort Worth AAF; he described it as "half a B-29 full." While a B-29 is a large airplane, it was designed to carry a load of heavy items—bombs—rather than a lot of lighter objects that might be carried by a cargoplane. Thus it would have been feasible to half-fill a B-29's storage area—its bomb bays—with no more debris than could have been stuffed into a station wagon and a Jeep Carry-All.

It isn't known how many airplanes left Roswell AAF carrying materials from the Corona crash site, or where all of them went. Wright Field (later Wright-Patterson Air Force Base) in Dayton, Ohio, is most often mentioned as the destination of one or more of these flights. Wright is a logical destination, as it housed much of the Army Air Forces' scientific laboratories and was staffed by some of the top technical people in the USAAF. But the details simply have not been unearthed.

There is reason to believe, however, that at least one airplane was sent down from Wright Field to either Roswell AAF or Fort Worth AAF to collect materials for return to Wright Field. The son of a man who was reportedly on such a flight told Stanton Friedman that it is his understanding that the crew actually played with some of the debris during the flight home.

It is known that not long after Marcel and Cavitt returned from the Foster ranch with their supply of fascinating debris, a much larger military force was sent to the ranch to collect every scrap. Residents have testified that Military Police set up roadblocks around the ranch and kept them away from the scene. They also kept the press out, as stated by Jud Roberts, then manager of radio station KGFL, in a 1990 interview:

"I wanted to go out to the crash site. [Station owner W. C.] Whitmore had been out there, but he couldn't get any closer than I did. I thought we could do it with back roads (of which the area is well supplied) but we didn't get close." They encountered Military Police who told them, "Sorry, but the road's closed. This is a restricted area." "It wasn't such a big deal, as we'd had these experiences before, when [airplane] accidents had happened. They just kind of blocked off the whole area. It was perfectly reasonable, as far as I was concerned. I'll bet I wasn't within fifteen miles [of the Foster ranch crash site]."

Even the limited evidence from the Corona area strongly suggests there were three separate crash sites: the so-called debris field on the Foster ranch, where so much scrap was found by Brazel and then collected by Marcel and Cavitt; a site several miles away, where the main body of the craft lay; and a site within a mile or two of that, where the bodies were found in or near what Glenn Dennis has described as "escape capsules."

Apparently the Roswell AAF mortuary officer had been

there, as had photographer F. B., who described the scene where he was taken to shoot pictures of bodies under the total control of an officer.

F. B. described another photographer being driven away to a different location where wreckage was being collected. This may have been the original "debris field," or it could have been the spot where what was left of the saucer ended up. Clearly, more information is needed from men who were there and who so far have refused to describe their experiences.

Next to nothing is known about the recovery of material and bodies from the San Agustin site, as the army did such an efficient job of sealing off the area. While it is not far from a paved road, it is in Catron County, the least heavily populated county in New Mexico, which in those days was one of the least populated of states. The closest thing to a description of post-crash activity comes from a diary kept by Jerry Anderson's uncle, Ted. While the copy of the diary acquired by Stanton Friedman through a complex series of negotiations is not an original (the ink did not exist in 1947), it may be one of several copies made by Ted or Victor in an effort to assure the information's survival. In it, he states:

> John T. and I talked on the phone and he said the Army is still out on the Plata [one of several local terms for the area] and they are combing the sand and putting stuff in bags and boxes and hauling it all away on big flat trailers. He said they have lights out there and all kinds of things. All the roads are blocked down there by the Army. John said they have machine guns and tanks and all that kind of stuff.
>
> John . . . said the Military is asking all kinds of questions up at Horse Springs store and Magdalena. Making a lot of noise about what could happen to traitors and that you could get shot for talking about military secrets.

It seems only logical that the material from the San Agustin crash could have gone to Alamogordo/White Sands, 150 miles to the southeast of the site, or perhaps to Kirtland AAF or Sandia Base at Albuquerque or even Los Alamos, north of Kirtland. All of these places were far better equipped to handle highly sensitive scientific materials than was Roswell. Witnesses claimed that some of the military people who arrived first at San Agustin were from Alamogordo.

The number of people involved in the recovery of wreckage and bodies, and the subsequent obliteration of clues to the crashes, was growing rapidly. Scores if not hundreds of men had been sent out from as many as four locations to the two crash sites to collect material, transport it, and guard against unauthorized intrusion and release of information. Once the material and bodies got back to the military facilities that had been hurriedly prepared to deal with this unprecedented challenge, more people joined the inner circle, and the job of security became even more complex.

The presence in New Mexico of very strange substances from the wreckage of the two crashes has been testified to by so many people that it is virtually proved. That the wreckage was accompanied by the bodies of as many as eight small humanoid aliens is another matter. A few people have described, in limited but highly consistent detail, their awareness or even direct observation of miniature, out-of-proportion bodies at the crash sites and elsewhere. The evidence for them is increasingly impressive, but perhaps not yet completely convincing.

However, like the acquisition of totally unfamiliar manufactured materials of striking physical characteristics, the confirmed existence of obviously nonhuman bodies will, by itself, establish not only the reality of UFOs but also their extraterrestrial origin. It is for this reason that so much effort has gone into trying to pin down the specifics of the reported observations, by Stanton Friedman and others. One of the most intriguing examples of secondhand testimony about alien bodies comes from a man who did not personally see them, but because of his unusual position was able to get close enough to realize that what was happening was very different from anything that had happened before.

Glenn Dennis was a young professional mortician in Roswell in the summer of 1947 whose employer, the Ballard

Funeral Home, had the contract with the Roswell Army Air Field to provide mortuary services. He drove a combination hearse and ambulance for both the civilian part of the business and the airbase assignments. On numerous occasions he had been called upon to help collect mangled bodies from military plane crashes and then prepare the remains for shipment back to the survivors. Dennis was fully familiar with the air base and "could go wherever I wanted to." It was this unusual ease of access to an otherwise secure military installation that enabled him to see and hear a lot more than he was supposed to.

In August 1989 Dennis was interviewed by Stanton Friedman in Lincoln, New Mexico, where he managed a historic tourist hotel. Even though the interview had to be squeezed into the turmoil of the annual celebration of Billy the Kid Day, Dennis was fully able to communicate the sense of excitement that surrounded his blundering into a particularly sensitive part of the Corona crash. Later he added information in other interviews.

The date was July 9 or 10, 1947. Glenn Dennis was as yet unaware of the discovery of the strange wreckage at the Foster ranch, and had heard nothing about alien bodies. He had gotten several puzzling phone calls from the Roswell AAF mortuary officer, who was more of an administrator than a technical specialist familiar with the intricacies of handling corpses, human or otherwise. The officer wanted to know about "hermetically sealed caskets: What was the smallest one they could get," Dennis recalled. Then he wanted to know "what the chemical solutions were that we were using for the vats and all that. He asked me about the chemical composition of blood, about the breakdown of tissue, what happened to tissue when it has laid out [in the sun] for several days."

This is what was so interesting. See, this is why I feel like there was really something involved in this, because they didn't want to do anything that was going to . . . make an imbalance. They kept saying, "OK, what's this going to do to the blood system, what's this going to do to the tissue?" Then when they informed me that these bodies [had] laid out in the middle of July, in the middle of the prairie, I mean that body's going to be as dark as your [blue] blazer, there, and it's going to be in bad shape. I was the one who suggested [using] dry ice . . . I'd done that a time or two.

I talked to them four or five times in the afternoon. They would keep calling back and asking me different questions involving the body. What they were really after was how to move those bodies. They didn't give me any indication they even had the bodies, or where they were. But they kept talking about these bodies, and I said, "What do the bodies look like?" And they said, "I don't know, but I'll tell you one thing: This happened some time ago." The only thing that was mentioned was that they were exposed to the elements for several days.

I understand these bodies weren't in the same location as where they found some of the others. They said the bodies weren't in the vehicle itself; the bodies were separated by two or three miles from it. They talked about three different bodies: two of them mangled, one that was in pretty good shape.

Later that day—around 6:00 or 7:00 P.M.—Dennis took a slightly injured GI accident victim to the base infirmary, which was in the same building as the hospital and the mortuary. He walked the airman inside and then drove around to the back of the building to see a pretty young Army Air Forces nurse he had recently gotten to know. He parked by the ramp as usual, next to several old-style, square military ambulances of World War II vintage. That was when things began to get sticky.

There were two MPs standing right there, and I got out and started to go in. I wouldn't have gotten as far as I did, if I hadn't parked in the Emergency area. They probably thought I was coming after somebody. The doors were open to the military ambulances and that's where some wreckage was, and there was an MP on each side. I saw all this wreckage.

I don't know what it was, but I knew there was something going on, and that's when I first got an inclination that something was happening. What was so curious about it, was that in two of those ambulances was a deal that looked like [the bottom] half of a canoe. It didn't look like aluminum . . . you know what stainless steel's like when you put heat on it? How it'll turn kinda purplish, with kind of a blue hue to it? [Glenn later said that he saw a row of unrecognizable symbols—several inches high—on the metal devices.] I just glanced in and kept going.

When I got inside, I noticed there was quite a bit of activity. When I went back into the lounge, there were "big birds" [high-ranking officers he didn't recognize, though he was familiar with all the local medical people] everywhere. They were really shook up. So I went down the hall where I usually go, and I got down the hall just a little way and an MP met me right there. He wanted to know who the hell I was and where I was from, and what business did I have there? I explained who I was. Evidently he was under the impression that they called me to come out.

Anyway, I got past that and I went on in and then this is where I met the nurse—she was involved in this thing, she was on duty. She told me, "How in the hell did you get in here?" I said, "I just walked in." She said, "My God, you are going to get killed!" And I said, "They didn't stop me!" I was going to the Coke machine to get us a Coke, and this big red-headed colonel said, "What's that son of a bitch doin' here?"

He hollered at the MPs and that's when it hit the fan! These two MPs grabbed me by the arms and carried me clear outside . . . they carried me to the ambulance . . . I didn't walk, they carried me! And they told me to get my ass out of there! [Not only that, but according to Dennis, they followed him all the way back to the funeral home.]

About two or three hours later, they [called] and told me, "You open your mouth [about this] and you'll be so far back in the jug they'll have to shoot pinto beans [into you] with a bean shooter!" I just laughed and said, "Go to hell!"

That was the last Glenn Dennis heard from anyone in an official position. He didn't see the nurse until the next day, and by then she was really upset. "She called me and said, 'If you've got time, come out. I need to talk to you.' " They agreed to meet at the officers' club for lunch, and when Dennis saw her, he was afraid she was about to go into shock, she looked so different. "My God, I don't know how you got in there," the nurse told him. "It's amazing what's going on. You wouldn't believe it! That's when she told me they did have some bodies. She said there were three little bodies; two of them were just mangled beyond everything, but there was one of them that was really in pretty good condition."

And she said, "Let me show you the difference between our anatomy and theirs. Really, what they looked like was ancient Chinese: small, fragile, no hair." She said their noses didn't protrude, the eyes were set pretty deep and the ears were just little indentations. She said the anatomy of the arms was different (the upper arm was longer than the lower). They didn't have thumbs, they had four different . . . she called them "tentacles," I think. Didn't have any fingernails. She then described how they had little things like suction cups on their fingertips.

I asked her were these men or women? [Were their] sex organs the same as ours? She said, "No, some were missing." [Dennis interjected, "The first thing that decomposes on a body would be the brain, next the sex organs, especially in women. But she thought there had probably been something . . . some animals. Some of these bodies were badly mutilated.

She said they got the bodies out of those containers [the ones he had seen in the backs of the ambulances, on the way into the hospital]. See, they weren't at the crash site, they were about a mile or two from the crash site. She said they looked like they had their own little cabins. She said the lower portion—the abdomen and legs—was crushed, but the upper portion wasn't that bad. She told me the head . . . was larger and it was kind of . . . like . . . the eyes were different.

The nurse then pulled out a prescription pad and drew some sketches of what she had described to Glenn Dennis. She gave him the drawings, warning him to keep them secret, and so he guarded them carefully. In 1990, he and Stanton Friedman went through his old files at the funeral home and discovered all his material had been thrown out several years before. Glenn then made some sketches of what he could remember.

"Until they got those bodies frozen, the smell was so bad you couldn't get within a hundred feet of them without gagging." It was when the nurse stepped out of the room where she had been assisting two doctors on the bodies, to get some air, that she had run into Dennis. She explained that even the doctors were getting sick, and that the smell was so bad they had to turn off the air conditioning to keep it from spreading throughout the hospital. Soon, they gave up trying to work under such conditions and completed the preparation of the bodies in a hangar.

After describing the strange events to Dennis, the nurse appeared to be on the verge of collapse from the emotional trauma, so he drove her back to her barracks. He never saw her again. Attempts to get in touch with her were met with obstruction. He was told she was away at a seminar, then that she had been transferred to England without even getting in touch with him. His first letter was answered with a cryptic promise from her to explain everything at a later date. His second letter was returned, stamped *Deceased*.

Efforts to trace the nurse have been unsuccessful. There is no file on her in the permanent military records office where all persons who have died while in service are supposed to be recorded. There is no evidence that anyone by her name served as an army nurse. Following a suggestion that she might have been killed in a military plane crash in England or Europe, a search was made of the newspaper *Stars and Stripes* as well as official records. If such a crash ever occurred, it has been wiped from the records.

A few weeks after the incident at the hospital, Glenn Dennis heard from his father: "What the hell'd you get into? What kind of trouble are you in?" I said, "I'm not in any trouble." And he said, "The hell you're not! The sheriff [an old friend of the elder Dennis] said that base personnel have been in and they want to know all about your background!" But there has never been any indication that the military did anything more about the uninvited mortician who got so close to the bodies. Dennis was a civilian who worked for a firm having a government contract, and was subject to military regulations only when he was on the airbase or on a military assignment such as an airplane crash recovery. Besides, he never saw a single alien body, though he must have been within a few feet of several of them.

One of the few people Glenn recognized in the hospital building during the brief, hectic period before he was forceably removed was a pediatrician who was then in the army. They talked several years later, when the man had returned to private practice. According to Dennis, "He didn't have a lot to say. We were pretty good friends. 'Hell,' he said, 'I don't know what it was. Whatever happened was completely out of my field of medicine.' " " 'That's what he told me,' " Dennis added. "But he was involved, and he and I discussed it."

Roswell was just a convenience. It was the military base down the street from the sheriff's office to which Mac Brazel brought his samples of material, and so it became a center of activity. But it was a flying field, not a scientific installation. If the materials and bodies recovered from the wilds were to be dealt with properly, they would have to be removed from Roswell AAF as quickly and as quietly, as possible.

Officers streamed into Roswell AAF from military bases around the country, shoved the local people out of the way and proceeded to turn the already secure airfield into an armed camp. People and buildings were commandeered as if nothing else in the world mattered, which just may have been the case. With an urgency borne of mystery and of pressure from the very top, Roswell AAF became the starting point for some unusual journeys.

It was necessary to ship every scrap of wreckage and at least three bodies and possibly one live alien to various installations where they could be handled and studied under conditions of greater security, and in more appropriate facilities. Roswell AAF would then have to be returned to its normal, precrash status as rapidly as possible, to reduce the chances of information leaking out and posing a serious threat to security.

The first flight out of Roswell with wreckage from the Foster ranch was probably on July 6 and consisted of the few pieces

Mac Brazel brought into town to show to Sheriff George Wilcox. It appears to have been flown to Fort Worth AAF and from there to Washington, but information on this is sketchy.

The next flight must have been on July 8, and carried the material brought back by Marcel and Cavitt. Retired M/Sgt. Robert Porter, a B-29 flight engineer with the 830th Bomb Squadron, related his part in this flight when interviewed during a conference of crash witnesses near Washington, D.C., in July 1990. He had talked to Friedman more than ten years before and is Loretta Proctor's brother.

> We flew these pieces—[some officers in the crew] told us it was parts of a flying saucer. The packages were in wrapping paper, one triangle-shaped about two and a half feet across the bottom, the rest in smaller, shoebox-sized packages. [They were in] brown paper with tape. It was just like I picked up an empty package . . . very light. The loaded triangle-shaped package and three shoebox-sized packages would have fit into the trunk of a car.
>
> On board were Lt. Col. Payne Jennings [deputy commander of Roswell] and Major Marcel. Captain Anderson said it was from a flying saucer. We got to Fort Worth, they transferred [the packages] to a B-25 and took them to Wright [Field]. When we landed at [Fort Worth], Colonel Jennings told us to take care of maintenance, and after a guard was posted, we could eat lunch. We came back, they told us they had transferred the material to a B-25. They told us it was a weather balloon. It *wasn't* a weather balloon!

There remains the discrepancy between Porter's description of just a few small packages of material on the flight carrying Major Marcel and the latter's statement to Stanton Friedman in 1979 that the load was "half a B-29 full." What is clear is that the material could hardly have been from something as ordinary, recognizable, and unmysterious as a weather balloon. Pieces of balloons are not transported with such urgency and security.

Another view of what was almost certainly the same flight comes from former 1st Lt. Robert Shirkey, then assistant opera-

tions officer of the 509th Bomb Group, who was also interviewed in July 1990. In July 1947 he was on duty in the Operations Office when things began to happen.

"A call came in to have a B-29 ready to go as soon as possible.
Where to? Fort Worth, on Colonel Blanchard's directive. [I was]
in the Operations Office when Colonel Blanchard arrived and
asked if the airplane was ready. When told it was, Blanchard
waved to somebody, and approximately five people came in the
front door, down the hallway and onto the ramp to climb into
the airplane, carrying parts of the crashed flying saucer. I got a
very short glimpse . . . asked Blanchard to turn sideways so [I]
could see, too. Saw them carrying pieces of metal: they had one
piece that was eighteen by twenty-four inches, brushed stainless steel in color." The plane went to Fort Worth and Marcel
went with it, Shirkey added.

There are certainly discrepancies, but after forty-three years,
memories begin to fade and to swirl together. While specific
details may vary, the general story is the same: A very special
flight was loaded with a small amount of material and sent to
Fort Worth under unusual and quite memorable conditions. It
was generally accepted that the material was from a crashed
flying saucer, though this was never put in writing or even
announced formally. Men who work close together, especially
in airplane crews, learn to communicate easily and to read
between the lines. They had been alerted to some very different
events by the Army's own security procedures.

One of the next flights to leave Roswell AAF was apparently
on or about July 9, according to former S/Sgt. Robert A. Slusher,
of the 393rd Bomb Squadron, who agreed to be interviewed in
early 1991. In midafternoon of that special day, he was aboard a
B-29 that taxied to the bomb-loading area, located far from the
main part of the base for safety reasons. There they loaded a
single crate he estimated was twelve feet long, five feet wide,
and four feet high.

There were MPs on board, Slusher said, and they were
armed, suggesting the crate contained something more exciting than canned hams or office supplies. Moreover, the four-

hundred-mile flight from Roswell AAF to Fort Worth AAF was at low level, four to five thousand feet. Usually, a B-29 on such a trip flies at twenty-five thousand feet, as its cabin is pressurized and a B-29 flies better at high altitude. But the bomb bay, where the mysterious crate was carried, cannot be pressurized, as it is designed to be opened in flight at high altitude so bombs can be dropped. Whatever was in the crate, which was too large to be carried in any other part of the airplane, had to be protected from a major drop in air pressure. Adding to the surreal atmosphere was the presence of the four MPs in the bomb bay.

When they arrived at Fort Worth AAF, 1st Lt. Felix Martucci of the 393rd Bomb Squadron told Slusher, "We made history." He did not elaborate, leaving the puzzled sergeant to make of it what he could. The crate was then loaded onto a flatbed weapons carrier and hauled off, accompanied by the MPs, whose need to guard a sealed wooden box was not explained.

On the flight back to Roswell, "Capt. Frederick Ewing was the pilot, the co-pilot was 1st Lt. Edgar Izard, Sgt. David Tyner was the engineer, the navigator was James Eubanks. Others involved were S/Sgt. Arthur Osepchook and Cpl. Thaddeus Love. The four MPs also came back with us.

"The return flight was above twenty thousand feet, and the cabin was pressurized. The round trip took approximately three hours, fifteen minutes. The flight was unusual in that we flew there, dropped the cargo, and returned immediately. It was a hurried flight; normally we knew the day before [that] there would be a flight.

"There was a rumor that the crate had debris from the crash. Whether there were any bodies, I don't know. The crate had been specially made; it had no markings."

By flying at low altitude with the special crate, the army planted the idea that whatever was in it, was sensitive to air pressure. That suggests it was not merely scrap pieces of metal brought back by Marcel and Cavitt but rather something biological, such as a body or even a living being. But this is only a supposition, based solely on circumstantial evidence.

Once the material returned to Roswell AAF by Marcel and Cavitt had been sent elsewhere, the army set out to collect what remained at the sheep ranch. A major recovery operation was put into motion, and a large quantity of foil, I beams, heavy paper, black plastic, and other materials were trucked the seventy-five difficult miles to Roswell. Robert E. Smith was then a member of the 1st Air Transport Unit, which operated Douglas C-54 Skymaster four-engined cargo planes out of the Roswell AAF. In a 1991 interview, he described his involvement:

A lot of people began coming in all of a sudden because of the official investigation. Somebody said it was a plane crash, but we heard from a man in Roswell that it was not a plane crash: it was something else, a strange object. There was another indication that something serious was going on. One night, when we were coming back to Roswell, a convoy of trucks covered with canvas passed us. When they got to the [airfield] gate, they headed over to this hangar on the east end, which was rather unusual. The truck convoy had red lights and sirens.

My involvement in the . . . incident was to help load crates of debris into the aircraft. We all became aware of the event when we went to the hangar on the east side of the ramp. There were a lot of people in plain clothes all over the place. They were "inspectors," but they were strangers on the base. When challenged, they replied they were here on Project So-and-So, and flashed a card, which was different from a military ID card.

We were taken to the hangar to load crates. There was a lot of farm dirt on the hangar floor. We loaded [the crates] on flatbeds and dollies; each crate had to be checked as to width and height. We had to know which crates went on which plane. We loaded crates on three [or] four C-54s. We weren't supposed to know their destination, but we were told they were headed north.

All I saw was a little piece of material. You could crumple it up, let it come out; you couldn't crease it. One of our people put it in his pocket. The piece of debris I saw was two to three inches square. It was jagged. When you crumpled it up, it then laid back out. And when it did, it kind of crackled, making a sound like celophane . . . it crackled when it was let out. There were no creases.

There were armed guards around during loading of our planes, which was unusual at Roswell. There was no way to get to the ramp except through armed guards. There were MPs on the outskirts, and our personnel were between them and the planes.

The largest [crate] was roughly twenty feet long, four to five feet high, and four to five feet wide. It took up an entire plane; it wasn't that heavy, but it was a large volume. The rest of the crates were two or three feet long and two feet square or smaller. The sergeant who had the piece of material said [it was like] the material in the crates. The entire loading took at least six, perhaps eight hours. Lunch was brought to us, which was unusual. The crates were brought to us on flatbed dollies, which was also unusual.

Officially, we were told it was a crashed plane, but crashed planes usually were taken to the salvage yard, not flown out. I don't think it was an experimental plane, because not too many people in that area were experimenting with planes. I'm convinced that what we loaded was a UFO that got into mechanical problems . . . even with the most intelligent people, things go wrong.

The C-54 into which Smith helped load the single twenty-foot crate "would have been Pappy Henderson's. I remember seeing T/Sgt. Harbell Elzey, T/Sgt. Edward Bretherton, and S/Sgt. William Fortner.

Capt. Oliver Wendell "Pappy" Henderson may have been the most highly regarded pilot at Roswell AAF. A veteran of thirty missions in B-24 Liberator bombers in Europe, he participated in the postwar A-bomb tests in the Pacific and earned major commendations for his flying. Henderson kept quiet about the unsettling events of July 1947 for three decades. Finally, he mentioned them to a fellow retired officer, dentist John Kromschroeder, with whom he was then involved in a joint business venture. The dentist said nothing about this until July 1990, more than four years after Henderson's death from cancer.

In 1977, Pappy had told Kromschroeder about the incident. He said he transported wreckage and alien bodies, describing the latter as "spacecraft garbage," and adding "the passengers suffered their death." Henderson, in the recollection of

Kromschroeder, described the bodies simply as being "small." About a year later, around 1978, Henderson produced a piece of metal he had taken from the collection of wreckage. "I gave it a good, thorough looking-at," Kromschroeder said in 1990, "and decided it was an alloy we are not familiar with (he and Henderson shared an interest in metallurgy). Gray, lustrous metal resembling aluminum, lighter in weight and much stiffer. [We couldn't] bend it . . . edges sharp and jagged."

The priceless scrap of material may be tucked away in Pappy's records and papers, just waiting to be freed. But there is currently no way to search the two thousand-plus cubic feet of materials that jam two small storage buildings and a garage to the ceilings. His widow, Sappho, has rejected suggestions that investigators be allowed to search through a lifetime of her late husband's memorabilia. The prospect is daunting, for a slim piece of metal could be hidden between any two pieces of paper in any of many scores of bulging cardboard boxes. Even if she were willing to have strangers paw through such personal matters, it could take hundreds of hours, and there is no assurance that the scrap of crashed UFO is there. It could have been lost, thrown out, or even confiscated.

In 1982, Henderson met with several members of his old bomber crew during an Air Division reunion in Nashville. According to one of the men in the group, "It was in his hotel room that he told us the story of the UFO and about his part. All we were told by Pappy is that he flew the plane to Wright Field. He definitely mentioned the bodies, but I don't recall any details except that they were small and different. I was skeptical at first, but soon saw that Pappy was quite serious."

Pappy died before Stanton Friedman got a chance to interview him. But his widow, Sappho, agreed to be interviewed, as did his daughter, Mary. Sappho described what her husband had told her:

We met during World War II when he flew with the 446th Bomb Squadron; he flew B-24s [on] thirty missions over Germany. After the war, he returned home . . . and was then sent to Roswell.

While stationed there, he ran the "Green Hornet Airline," which involved flying C-54s and C-47s carrying VIPs, scientists, and materials from Roswell to the Pacific during the atom bomb tests. He had to have a Top Secret clearance for this responsibility.

In 1980 or 1981, he picked up a newspaper at a grocery store where we were living in San Diego. One article described the crash of a UFO outside Roswell, with the bodies of aliens discovered beside the craft. He pointed out the article to me and said, "I want you to read this article, because it's a true story. I'm the pilot who flew the wreckage of the UFO to Dayton, Ohio [home of Wright Field]. I guess now that they're putting it in the paper, I can tell you about this. I wanted to tell you for years." Pappy never discussed his work because of his security clearance.

He described the beings as small with large heads for their size. He said the material that their suits were made of was different than anything he had ever seen. He said they looked strange. I believe he mentioned that the bodies had been packed in dry ice to preserve them.

Mrs. Mary Kathryn Groode, Pappy's daughter, added her remembrances to those of her mother.

When I was growing up, he and I would often spend evenings looking at the stars. On one occasion, I asked him what he was looking for. He said, "I'm looking for flying saucers. They're real, you know."

In 1981, during a visit to my parents' home, my father showed me a newspaper article which described the crash of a UFO and the recovery of alien bodies outside Roswell, New Mexico. He told me that he saw the crashed craft and the alien bodies described in the article, and that he had flown the wreckage to Ohio. He described the alien beings as small and pale, with slanted eyes and large heads. He said they were humanoid-looking, but different from us. I think he said there were three bodies.

He said the matter had been Top Secret and that he was not supposed to discuss it with anyone, but that he felt it was alright to tell me because it was in the newspaper.

Friedman also spoke with Pappy's son and cousin, both of whom told of having heard Pappy quietly tell his story after the newspaper article appeared.

On the basis of all that is known of Pappy's brief mentions of his involvement with the events at Roswell, it appears that while he probably saw bodies at the airbase, he may have transported only materials to Wright Field.

Another man who saw bodies was Sgt. Melvin Brown, a cook at Roswell AAF who was called out to help guard the material retrieved from the Foster ranch. In 1989, his daughter Beverly gave the following story to Stanton Friedman from her home in England, about her late father, "Brownie":

When we were young, he used to tell us stories about things that had happened to him when he was young. We got to know those stories by heart and would all say together, "Here we go again!"

Sometimes, but not too often, he used to say that he saw a man from outer space. That used to make us all giggle like mad. He said he had to stand guard duty outside a hangar where a crashed flying saucer was stored, and that his commanding officer said, "Come on, Brownie, let's have a look inside." But they didn't see anything because it had all been packed up and [was] ready to be flown out to Texas.

He also said that one day all available men were grabbed and that they had to stand guard where a crashed disc had come down. Everything was being loaded onto trucks, and he couldn't understand why some of the trucks had ice or something in them. He did not understand what they wanted to keep cold. Him and another guy had to ride in the back of one of the trucks, and although they were told that they could get into a lot of trouble if they took in too much of what was happening, they had a quick look under the covering and saw two dead bodies ... alien bodies.

We really had to giggle at that bit. He said they were smaller than a normal man—about four feet—and had much larger heads than us, with slanted eyes, and that the bodies looked yellowish, a bit Asian-looking. We did not believe him when we were kids, but as I got older, I did kind of believe it. Once I asked him if he was scared by them, and he said, "Hell no, they looked nice, almost as though they would be friendly if they were alive."

The descriptions of bodies are not merely highly consistent, but agree in most respects with those given by persons suspected of having been "abducted" by presumed aliens. Moreover, the same general descriptions of aliens can be found in most reports from people claiming to have seen them near their landed UFOs, in what has come to be known as "Close Encounters of the Third Kind."

The total of aliens recovered from the two crashes may be as high as eight: three dead and perhaps one live one from the Foster Ranch crash, and three dead and one live from the Plains of San Agustin crash. Regardless of the total, there had to be sufficient body parts to keep a crew of top medical people busy for a very long time dissecting, analyzing, theorizing, and then writing about the most momentous event in the history of the biological sciences.

Keeping such information secret from the scientific community might be considered an act of unconscionable malfeasance, as it is quite possible that the widespread dissemination of this information could have led to major advances in medical and other sciences. Moreover, if even one alien remained alive long enough for even the simplest of communication to be established, the increase in general knowledge could have been amazing. Unfortunately, the government's insistence on absolute secrecy has prevented the world from participating in a rare opportunity for increased knowledge.

10

The Great Cover-up

THE UFO CRASHES in New Mexico launched the U.S. government on a long-term, elaborate, and highly sophisticated campaign of concealment and disinformation that has yet to be relaxed. Could it have sprung spontaneously from the first strange-sounding report of some unusual events in the wilds of New Mexico? Could the government have been capable of instantly springing into action to cut off all news of the crashes even before most of the details were known? Could a lot of otherwise cautious and conservative generals and politicians in Washington have been completely convinced of the totally exotic nature of the crash remains and spontaneously grasped the staggering significance of the events?

When Lydia Sleppy was told by telephone (around 4:00 P.M. on July 7) by Roswell radio station manager Johnny McBoyle that he had been to a crash site and seen the wreckage, this was the first that anyone in the public arena had heard. Mac Brazel had shown a small amount of debris to Sheriff Wilcox in Roswell, and this led to the trip of Maj. Jesse Marcel and Capt. Sheridan Cavitt of the Counter-Intelligence Corps to the Foster ranch crash site. But the two government men were either still out there or on their way back, over poor roads and through almost-uninhabited country, when the teletype message was interrupted by someone who obviously knew that something very important and sensitive was going on.

How could anyone in a position of authority in New Mexico or Washington, D.C., have known that McBoyle was telling Mrs. Sleppy about the nature of one of the crashes? Or that she was trying to send the story out over a press teletype machine? And that the story was both true and earthshaking?

Could Major Marcel's brief conversation with his commanding officer, Colonel Blanchard, have triggered an alert at higher headquarters, which the latter may have notified? But Blanchard was the man who ordered 1st. Lt. Walter Haut, Roswell AAF public information officer, to issue a press release, around noon of the day *after* the mysterious teletype interference, that the army had recovered the remains of a crashed flying disc. His notification of higher headquarters, if it indeed ever happened, must not have produced the degree of concern that would have led to an order to "cease transmission" received by Mrs. Sleppy on the afternoon of July 7. If it had, Colonel Blanchard would certainly have been ordered to refrain from letting the word out, though he might not have been told exactly why it was so important to keep quiet. Had he released the information after being told not to, his career would have been placed in jeopardy, rather than kept on a track which eventually made him one of the Air Force's top generals.

It is clear that some sort of system must already have been in place in Washington which reached out to all parts of the United States, including such spots as Roswell, New Mexico. (In 1947, Roswell was even smaller than it is today, with barely 25,000 residents. It was a little town with a very secret air base.) The system had to involve monitoring (possibly outside the law) of telephone calls and teletype wires. Today, the National Security Agency (NSA) may be able to do this sort of thing with relative ease, thanks to billions of dollars spent on terribly advanced electronic gadgets. But this happened back in 1947, before there was an NSA and before most cities even had commercial television. Many homes in rural New Mexico were still years away from telephone service.

A monitoring/surveillance system extensive enough to do this kind of job had to be very expensive, and spending at this level (at least in those days) implies an exceptionally important purpose. It could not have been created overnight, on a whim. Obviously, something powerful must have convinced the president of the United States (Harry Truman or even Franklin D. Roosevelt) that it was absolutely essential to achieve total control of any new UFO crashes before word leaked out to the public.

A few sightings reported in the newspapers or on radio, especially those from ordinary citizens, could hardly have led to the creation of such a system (though they might have activated one already in place). Nor could some sightings by airline or military pilots have catapulted government officials straight from gross ignorance to total acceptance, because the first flying saucer wave was barely two weeks old. For much of that time, the average citizen had been snickering over the reports, and sophisticated national leaders were no doubt laughing out loud. It had to be something much more tangible, more specific, and more impressive that convinced the Pentagon and the White House that instant action was vital.

Something like an earlier crash whose wreckage had been recovered and studied by government scientists. Or proof of the unique and important nature of the World War II foo fighters, no official report of which has ever been released. Or something discovered during the 1946 Swedish ghost rocket sighting wave. Remember, Gen. Jimmy Doolittle played a role in the American part of both these "proto-UFO" waves. As one of the most respected men in American official and scientific life, (he received the first Ph.D. in aeronautics) his opinions and advice would have carried great weight. And he had direct access to the White House.

Whatever it was that impressed a lot of otherwise pretty blasé high government officials with the unprecedented nature of what was flying around, it must have been hardware, bodies, or something else equally unambiguous. Some thick, hard-to-read scientific report could hardly have done the trick. But exactly what carried the day has yet to be hinted at.

Given that members of some special security team might well have been sitting on the edges of their chairs in Washington at the time the first word was received of the New Mexico crashes, how was it that news of the recovery of wreckage from the sheep ranch was allowed to get out via an official Army Air Forces news release? Was it a slip-up? Or might it have been the inevitable consequence of an unusually secretive process?

The news that a system existed for detecting alien crashes and then controlling all information about them would, of necessity, have to be kept secret from almost everyone in the government as well as outside it. Otherwise, the importance of the subject of alien spacecraft could become common knowledge, and the chances of maintaining control would be seriously diminished. That the very idea was given credence had to be kept secret.

Such a system involves and illustrates the nature of the intelligence practice of compartmentalization. To operate effectively, especially vital information must be kept in a special "compartment," access to which is limited to those who have a specific, demonstrable "need to know" that particular information in order to do their jobs. Everyone else, no matter what their exalted rank or position, does not qualify, regardless of the security clearances they may possess. The situation of former U.S. senator Barry Goldwater (R., Ariz.) offers a prime example. Even though he was a general in the U.S. Air Force Reserve and chairman of the powerful Senate Armed Services Committee, he was unable to break through the wall of secrecy surrounding the government's UFO information and activity. This clearly upset him, but not even his considerable influence was sufficient to provide him with a need to know that particular category of sensitive information.

It is quite possible that not a single person at Roswell Army Air Field had a need to know about the nature of the flying saucers. And so, when Marcel and Cavitt returned from the Foster ranch with a lot of material like the odd samples Marcel had seen at the sheriff's office, Colonel Blanchard had no reason to refrain from telling Lieutenant Haut to issue a press release about it. His ignorance of the inner workings of the situation resulted from a necessary element of the security process.

Someone clearly had gotten wind of the discovery of crash wreckage at the sheep ranch several hours before Marcel and Cavitt had finished collecting debris, or at least while they were on their way back to Roswell with it. Could it have been that CICman Cavitt called his immediate superiors (not at Roswell, but at Albuquerque or even Washington) just as soon as Major Marcel described the strange material to him by phone while telling him they were going out to the ranch to collect more? Cavitt could easily have been part of a system set up to alert some special, secret office to flying saucer crashes, even if he didn't know why it was so important.

Cavitt is one of the few people still living who were involved in the retrieval of crash materials and who would have known a lot of details, rather than just a small part of the story. He is also one of two key witnesses who refuses to say anything; the other is the air base provost marshal—who, when called, said he could not talk because he signed a security oath back in 1947. Cavitt has even tried to deny being near a crash site, even though his assistant, Bill Rickett, and Maj. Jesse Marcel have placed him at the site and deeply involved in the operation.

Or it could have been that the discovery of a complete craft at the Plains of San Agustin even before the government learned of the debris at the sheep ranch could have initiated the rapid response of a team of specialists who had been poised for just such a call since the flying saucer wave of 1947 began, if not earlier. They could have immediately begun tapping telephone and teletype lines and monitoring radio stations around New Mexico. Maintaining surveillance of the state's many newspapers would have been a lot more difficult and would have increased the risk of public exposure, as it could only have been achieved on the scene by a lot of people. This could have led to the rapid and widespread coverage of Lieutenant Haut's news release. Radio stations outside New Mexico could have picked up the story from newspapers or the wire services, resulting in broadcasts such as the one heard by Hughie Green and one of the authors.

In the aftermath of the crashes, studies were begun by the U.S. Army Air Forces which were aimed at learning if the saucers were real and, if so, what they were, where they were from, who was flying them, and so on. But if wreckage (not to say bodies) had already been retrieved and seen to be so far from the norm that their extraterrestrial origin was obvious, why was anyone bothering with studies that had already been superseded?

The Eisenhower briefing paper suggests an answer, as does the fact that the matter would unquestionably have been very highly classified. "These [flying saucer] reports resulted in independent efforts by several different elements of the military to ascertain the nature and purpose of the objects," the paper says. Could it have been that while the supersecret "saucer crash office" was fully aware of the nature of the saucers, it had to keep its information secret even from other parts of the Army Air Forces?

The next indication of Washington's awareness of and concern for what was happening came on the afternoon of Tuesday, July 8. At Eighth Air Force Headquarters in Fort Worth, Texas, the phone rang in the office of Col. (later Brig. Gen.) Thomas J. DuBose, chief of staff to Eighth Air Force Commander Gen. Roger Ramey. At the other end was Gen. Clemence McMullen, calling from Washington. He ordered Colonel DuBose to tell (not to ask) General Ramey to send some of the material immediately to Washington and to hush up any stories about the army recovering a crashed flying saucer by concocting a cover story to "get the press off our backs."

"Do you understand me, Colonel?"

"Yes, sir!" DuBose replied.

DuBose quickly passed the word to his boss, General Ramey, and as soon as the four-engined bomber arrived from Roswell Army Air Field with its load of debris ("about half a B-29 full," according to Maj. Jesse Marcel), Ramey took over. He ordered the material sent on to Washington and he told Marcel to speak to no one about his experience and to return to Roswell. As a loyal and realistic officer, Marcel did exactly that.

General Ramey invited the press in to announce that the excitement was over, and that the wreckage found on the Foster ranch was nothing more than the remains of the radar reflector from a rawinsonde weather balloon. To do this in a convincing manner, he had someone find just such a device, made certain it looked badly damaged and presented it to the press. He then called in Warrant Officer Irving Newton from the base weather office, who promptly and correctly identified it as a weather balloon and its radar reflector.

The press obligingly took notes and photographs of General Ramey and Major Marcel, and quickly put the story out on the wires: The "crashed flying saucer" was no more than a weather balloon that had been misidentified by the rancher and the first military people to see it. Major Marcel had been ordered to keep quiet, and Captain Cavitt was nowhere to be seen. The military people who could easily have spilled the beans had thus been taken care of.

It should be noted here that, due to the brief window of opportunity between Walter Haut's press release (at noon, Albuquerque time) and Ramey's official explanation a few hours later, the only newspapers that carried the crashed-saucer recovery story were evening papers from the Midwest to the West, such as the Chicago *Daily News*, the Los Angeles *Herald Express*, the San Francisco *Examiner*, and the Roswell *Daily Record*. Major newspapers like the New York *Times*, the Washington *Post*, and the Chicago *Tribune* were morning papers and so carried only the cover-up story the next morning.

Next on the list of potential threats to the government's plan was William "Mac" Brazel, who may not have had much technical background, but clearly knew a weather balloon when he saw one. More important, he could describe the wreckage in sufficient detail to convince almost anyone that it was very unusual stuff.

The military took Brazel into custody for about a week,

during which time he was seen on the streets of Roswell with an official escort. While his behavior aroused the curiosity of friends when he passed them without any sign of recognition, none was motivated to do or say anything about it. Military secrecy was a way of life in New Mexico in those days (and still is, to a considerable extent), and even civilians having no connection to the government were security-conscious and assumed the government had good reasons for doing whatever it was doing.

Just what techniques the USAAF used on Mac Brazel to keep him from talking are not known. But they were effective, as there is no suggestion that he said anything substantive on the subject for the rest of his life. Several people have testified that right after the event, Mac seemed to have a lot more money than usual, suggesting he was either given a lump sum or something in the nature of a pension. He is reported to have bought a new truck and then left the ranching business to open a public cold storage locker. But others who knew him insist Mac would never have submitted to bribery.

The military continued to keep an eye on civilians in the area. A casual remark by Bill Brazel in a recreation hall a few weeks after the crash led to the confiscation of a cigar box full of small bits of wreckage.

When it came to civilians who had even indirect knowledge of the recovery of bodies, the military was a lot tougher. It went so far as to threaten witnesses with jail if they talked, and even hinted that their families might be placed in jeopardy.

The press was not spared, either. Calls were made to Roswell radio stations, allegedly from New Mexico politicians in Washington, which made it clear that FCC licenses would be canceled promptly if secrecy was not maintained. More than one case of reporter's notes vanishing from desk drawers has been reported. Today, such behavior on the part of the federal government would almost certainly backfire and lead to protests and even exposés. But in the New Mexico of 1947, the atmosphere was one of total, unquestioning cooperation with the government, even if the principles of a free press had to be compromised.

As a result of unprecedented cover-up and censorship efforts, the story of the crashes in New Mexico remained totally secret for more than thirty years, and effectively secret for more than forty. There are those who insist that the U.S. government is incapable of keeping secrets, offering as evidence the many leaks that have been given heavy press coverage. True enough, but the secrets that *are* kept are those of which the public knows nothing. An official of the U.S. National Archives told the authors that he is aware of classified documents dating back to the *First* World War! Both authors handled materials classified top secret and higher, Friedman when in the nuclear industry and Berliner when in the air force. Both are aware of the procedures involved in protecting such material, and the ease with which highly classified documents can be kept secret. The only way classified materials can become known to the press and thus to the public is by those charged with their care leaking them. There is no way to pinpoint secrets which have been kept, and so only those broken are known.

A variety of objections to the above notions are frequently offered by persons apparently not familiar with the world of classified documents and projects:

1. OBJECTION: Surely all classified documents are eventually declassified within twenty years, or at most thirty or even forty years. Therefore, any documents relating to the New Mexico crashes, if they existed at all, would now be available.

RESPONSE: There is no general requirement for automatic declassification of all documents, though some are so labeled. As an example, in 1990 the Truman Library reviewed its files of the CIA's Psychological Strategy Board. Half the material could not be declassified for "national security reasons" even though all of it pre-dated 1953.

To cite another example: Friedman requested access to material at the National Archives in the Air Force Headquarters file, all of it from 1956 or earlier. He was allowed to see less than 10 percent of it.

2. OBJECTION: It would be impossible to keep crashes secret,

with so many people allegedly knowing bits and pieces of the story. Someone would have talked.

RESPONSE: Many people *have* talked about what little they know, though key people like CICman Cavitt continue to stonewall. Tens of billions of dollars are spent each year by hundreds of thousands of people to keep secrets, and much of this effort is 100 percent successful.

3. OBJECTION: There is no way the government could hide the wreckage of a crashed saucer, or alien bodies.

RESPONSE: Obviously, our stockpiles of nuclear weapons, chemical and biological agents, high-tech equipment, laser weapons, and the like are kept well hidden. Considering that the United States has an estimated twenty thousand nuclear warheads, then hiding a saucer or two with a few bodies would not be difficult. There are thousands of square miles in the American West that are off limits to private and commercial aircraft, and a large area near Nellis AFB, Nevada, is forbidden even to most military flights.

4. OBJECTION: The Freedom of Information Act has made it possible for any citizen to get any document, and federal agencies have to respond promptly to all requests. If crash-related documents ever existed, they would have to be released under this system.

RESPONSE: Each agency has many categories of information it need not release. Furthermore, documents usually have to be carefully identified, which makes general requests almost useless. Requests often take several years to fulfill, especially when they are made to the CIA or NSC. It took Friedman five years to get a few small portions of old CIA documents, many of which turned out to be translated European newspaper articles. Half his requests were turned down flat, and many others were answered with pages almost entirely blacked out. (See appendices.)

5. OBJECTION: While it might be possible to hide saucers and

bodies, it would not be possible to move a large, intact saucer cross-country without people becoming aware of it.

RESPONSE: In 1945, a 240-ton steel cylinder was moved overland from Ohio to Trinity Site in New Mexico for the first atomic bomb test. If anyone paid much attention to the huge contraption, no evidence of it can be found today. Now, nuclear weapons and bomb components are routinely shipped around the country in secret.

11

Alternative Explanations for the Wreckage

O THER EXPLANATIONS have been offered for what crashed in New Mexico, starting with the official cover story of the weather balloon. More recently, alternative explanations have been proposed by writers on both sides of the UFO-reality debate, in some cases because general acceptance of the nature of the crashes would repudiate their own theories and published writings. But if what crashed in New Mexico weren't alien craft, what were they?

Several other explanations have been offered for the strange materials and even for the bodies of miniature humanoids, which many people have testified were recovered from two widely separated crash sites at about the same time. Actually, these terrestrial explanations are for the Corona site wreckage only, as what was allegedly found at the Plains of San Agustin was clearly alien.

While the authors find none of these alternate explanations particularly convincing, they deserve to be mentioned in the cause of objectivity.

AMERICAN TEST ROCKET

Several people have seriously suggested that all that was found at the Foster ranch was the remains of one of the captured German-built V-2 unguided ballistic missiles known to have been test-fired from the White Sands proving ground, less than a hundred miles southwest of Corona, New Mexico. This might account for the finding of a lot of unfamiliar parts. And while it could have initially fooled sheep rancher Mac Brazel, it could hardly have posed much of a mystery for Maj. Jesse Marcel, whose years in Army Air Forces Intelligence had brought him into contact with, or at least awareness of, a wide variety of common and uncommon air and space devices.

Moreover, the presence of part numbers and writing on pieces of wreckage, even if in German, would quickly have revealed the smashed bits as something known. The presence of unknown and unreadable symbols, on the other hand, would have pointed away from the wreckage being that of a V-2. The latter was the case. Chinese or Japanese symbols would have been recognized as such, as would Cyrillic, even if they could not be read. Major Marcel commented that the symbols looked something like Egyptian hieroglyphics, but one is hard pressed to imagine an ancient Egyptian rocket or airplane being flown over New Mexico in 1947.

As for the bodies that were found some distance from the debris field, some proponents of the rocket explanation suggest they were nothing more exotic than rhesus monkeys that had been lofted into near-space as part of a biological test program that would eventually lead to manned space flight. But rhesus monkeys, no matter how badly battered by the force of a crash, would still have looked enough like monkeys to have been recognized as such by the first experts to see them. And since the first V-2 carrying a live monkey (in Project Blossom) did not lift off until June 11, 1948, and then carried only one (named Albert), a crash eleven months earlier could hardly have been such a test.

The big question of course remains: Why would the crash of

a test V-2, with or without monkeys, have been treated as a military secret of epic proportions? Other rocket test mishaps, with and without passengers, were publicized with no great harm resulting. If the wreckage had been nothing more extreme than this, it would certainly have been announced as such, and the entire matter completely defused for all time. The crash of an errant V-2 near the town of Jaurez, Mexico, a few weeks earlier (May 29, 1947) wasn't kept secret.

By handling the story as it did, the U.S. government provided the best possible reason for concluding that what crashed was truly mysterious.

JAPANESE BOMB-CARRYING BALLOON

This is the most recently concocted explanation for the Corona crash, and makes no more sense than does the V-2 rocket explanation, and for some of the same reasons.

From November 1944, through April 1945, the Japanese launched more than nine thousand crude, gas-filled balloons, each carrying fifty to seventy-five pounds of incendiary or high-explosive bombs. As many as a thousand of them may have ridden the prevailing winds all the way to North America. Damage from the bombs was limited to a few small fires and the deaths of six overly inquisitive people on an outing who came across one in the woods.

The balloons were thirty-three feet in diameter, made of laminated paper or rubberized silk, and carried a payload of more than three hundred pounds, most of which was the mechanism which controlled the balloon's altitude as it drifted along. In order to frustrate the Japanese in their efforts to learn how effective the novel weapon was, the U.S. clamped down on news coverage and thus kept locations of the landings secret until the tragedy of May 1945. By then, launches had ceased due to the impact of American bombing raids on the manufacturing and launching facilities in Japan.

That the materials found on Foster Ranch could have been from such a balloon and its payload is very hard to swallow.

The last launch from Japan was in early April 1945, more than two years before the discovery of the wreckage. Where had the balloon been in the meantime? Not on the ranch, or Mac Brazel would surely have seen it many times. Could it somehow have been in flight all that time? At the average speed these balloons traveled, it would have made thirty-three trips around the world! With an altitude-controlling mechanism designed for, at most, one week of descending, dropping one or two sandbags, and then climbing back up to its cruising altitude, the balloon would have needed divine intervention to remain in flight until July 1947.

Moreover, the wreckage, according to those who saw it, did not include a single scrap of anything similar to the remains of a Japanese balloon, many of which had been recovered by the military and civilians in the final months of World War II and thereafter. The payload section, for instance, was quite ordinary in appearance, being composed of conventionally shaped bits of inexpensive metal. While its purpose might not have been immediately obvious, its Japanese origin would have been revealed quickly. Hundreds of others had been rapidly identified . . . why not this one?

The balloon bombs had not been a matter of military security since the May 22, 1945, joint announcement by the War and Navy departments that let the American people in on the scheme.

WEATHER BALLOON

This was the original cover story created by the brass at Fort Worth Army Air Field and is still repeated, despite its inability to account for the reported characteristics of the recovered materials. A rawinsonde balloon carries a flimsy, hexagonal, foil-and-wood, kitelike contraption intended to reflect radar and thus make it easier to track the balloon.

But what was found on the Foster ranch was 100-percent unfamiliar materials having particularly impressive physical qualities. There was no rubberized balloon fabric, no aluminized mylar, no wooden sticks, no labels identifying it as the property of the U.S. Weather Bureau or some military weather service. It was just superlight, superstrong pieces of thin skin, of slender I beams, of parchmentlike substance, and of black plastic.

To make this explanation worth considering seriously, one would have to accept that Mac Brazel was unable to recognize ordinary weather-balloon materials. Yet he stated that he knew what such balloons looked like, had recovered more than one, and was certain this was not such a device. He was not a stupid man, nor was Maj. Jesse Marcel or others who saw the wreckage at the crash site, or soon afterward when the first loads were brought to Roswell Army Air Field. If Major Marcel had been so naive that he failed to identify pieces of a simple, common weather balloon's reflector that was hardly worth a hurried trip to a remote sheep ranch on a Sunday afternoon, would he have been promoted shortly thereafter and given a much more important and sensitive job?

AMERICAN SECRET WEAPON

There is always the possibility that what crashed on the Foster ranch and even at the Plains of San Agustin was connected to the test flight of a secret American airplane or missile. This would account for its not being recognized by Mac Brazel, and for the way the entire episode was hushed up. At any one time, secret vehicles are being tested in the wide open spaces of the West where the chances of their being seen accidentally are at a minimum. This was true in 1947 and it is certainly true today.

But what was being tested in 1947 is not secret today. Either it met its requirements and was placed in production, or it failed in one or more ways and was sent to the scrap heap. Regardless, it would have been declassified and long since would have become common knowledge. By now, even if it had been totally successful, it would have been rendered obsolete by subsequent developments. Any remaining examples would probably be in museums. In 1947, the USAAF was very quietly testing the Bell XS-1 rocketplane (which would gain fame as the X-1 in which Chuck Yeager became the first man to fly faster than the speed of sound on October 14, 1947). In July 1947 it was very secret. Today it hangs in the Milestones of Flight hall of the National Air and Space Museum in Washington, D.C. Nothing about it remains secret: not its shape, nor its power, nor its construction, nor its performance.

In 1947, airplanes being tested at Muroc Army Air Field in southern California included the Northrop XB-35 flying wing heavy bomber, Convair XB-36 super-heavy bomber, North American XF-86 Sabre jet fighter, and Douglas D-558-I Skystreak research jet. None of these was ever involved in a mysterious crash, nor was one flown as far afield as New Mexico.

If what crashed in New Mexico in 1947 had been some secret American craft being tested, it would have been revealed as such many years ago and the mystery would have been solved to everyone's satisfaction. But what was so strange about the finding at the sheep ranch was not its radical configuration (it was just scrap which suggested no particular shape) but its composition. The materials were limited to those having very unusual weight, strength, and markings. Had such materials been available to American aircraft and missile manufacturers in the late 1940s and afterward, they would have replaced the relatively inferior aluminum alloys, titanium, special steels, and finally the advanced composites such as carbon fiber. Using materials of lesser quality when superior materials are available makes absolutely no sense. Not even under conditions of excessive security.

SECRET SOVIET WEAPON

This explanation has even more holes in it than the American secret weapon explanation. In addition to all the reasons listed immediately above can be added the now-obvious inability of 1947 Soviet technology to have produced anything half so advanced as what crashed in New Mexico. At the time, there was serious concern that the Soviets might have leaped far ahead using captured Nazi German technology and scientists. But that is no longer considered realistic, especially in view of our thorough knowledge of early Soviet jet airplanes and rockets.

Moreover, it makes absolutely no sense for the Soviets (or anyone else) to fly secret experimental (and therefore highly sensitive) aircraft over the United States, where the slightest malfunction would lead to a forced landing or a crash. Priceless secrets and a clear picture of the state of the art would have been revealed, and nothing would have been gained. We test our secret aircraft over the empty areas of Nevada and California, where they will attract minimum attention. The Soviets tested theirs over equally vacant parts of their huge country.

Having thus eliminated all the suggested alternative explanations for what was recovered from the New Mexico crash sites *does not* prove that alien spacecraft were responsible. There may yet be other explanations—obscure, yet mundane—that should be considered. One of them may provide the elusive solution to the questions that remain unanswered. After all, the process of elimination works *only* when you are absolutely certain you have considered all the possibilities.

There is one more possibility: that all the witnesses— military and civilian—are lying. Accusations are not enough. Proof must be presented that dozens of persons with excellent reputations in their communities have conspired to invent a complex story for no apparent reason. Lacking such proof, it must be assumed that the witnesses are telling the truth as they remember it.

12

Keeping the Secret

FOR MORE THAN forty years the U.S. government has kept the nature of the UFO crashes in New Mexico sufficiently secret to make it appear that they never happened. For that matter, it has been able to keep the American people from learning much about UFOs in general, even though hundreds of thousands have seen them, and a majority is convinced they are real and probably extraterrestrial.

This almost certainly constitutes the greatest example of secret-keeping in history. It far outclasses even the landmark job done to conceal the development of the first atomic bomb in the early 1940s, for that security operation was during wartime and represented the collective will of the nation. And the secret was kept for just a few years, at that.

The story of the reality and nature of UFOs has been kept under wraps for almost half a century, during no fewer than nine different presidential administrations, several major wars, and the flowering of manned space travel. Even while the American people were becoming world- and space-conscious, their government's attitude toward UFOs remained intractable and secure.

When UFOs burst upon the scene in late June 1947, they were publicly held up to ridicule and in private frantically researched. The initial (and perfectly reasonable) fear that they might be unexpectedly advanced Soviet airplanes or missiles

148

was quickly replaced by concern that the public might panic if rumors of "little green men from Mars" were allowed to circulate.

Before much could be learned from early reports of sightings of flying saucers, at least one of them crashed and revealed many of its secrets to a carefully controlled group of government people. While the public was still being led to believe that the saucers they were seeing were nothing more than clouds and airplanes and balloons, there were people in Washington and at Wright Field who knew they were not only real, but extraterrestrial. The decision was made by the White House to keep all this utterly private.

The 1947 wave of flying saucer sightings produced enough spontaneous ridicule from the press and from scientists to convince most people that UFOs were pure imagination. There was no need for the government to take any action to reduce the interest in the saucers as long as there was no sign anyone was taking them seriously.

When wreckage and bodies were recovered from the New Mexico crash sites and quickly identified as unearthly, orders blasted out of Washington to create a cover story, lest word get out that the Earth was playing involuntary host to unusual visitors. The press gratefully accepted the explanation that it had been nothing more exciting than the radar reflector from a wandering weather balloon and passed it along to millions of eager readers and listeners who were already convinced the flying saucers were kind of funny.

The effectiveness of the crash cover story was nothing short of amazing. More than thirty years passed before anyone paid attention to this vaguely reported event. Of course, there was limited basis for investigating the initial story of a crash and retrieval, inasmuch as so little information was available, and nothing else that had happened suggested there was any substance to flying saucer crash stories. But there were some clues that should have alerted a sharp reporter at the time, or some of the pioneering private UFO investigators when they first began to look into the mystery in the mid-1950s.

In the Washington *Post* for July 9, 1947 (the day after Lieutenant Haut's news release had triggered a short-lived flurry of
interest), was this reference to the cover story: "Brazell [sic]
found the broken remains of the weather device scattered over
a square mile of his land."

A square mile? How does a little weather balloon and its
flimsy, box kitelike radar reflector become spread out over
more than six hundred acres? When a weather balloon comes
to earth, it is either because it has developed a slow leak and
cannot maintain its altitude or because it has gone too high,
split, and let its helium gas escape more rapidly. Either way, the
balloon descends in a pretty leisurely fashion. Disabled balloons do not come hurtling to earth like diving airplanes or
reentering spacecraft. They float or flutter down, doing precious little damage to themselves or to anything on the ground
when they hit.

If the balloon, or what was left of it, had no choice but to
alight gently, what could have caused its payload to smash into
so many pieces that they could cover a square mile of sheep
ranch? Obviously, nothing! The metal foil and sticks that made
up the radar reflector would have been bent or even broken,
while the balloon itself would almost certainly have still been
in one piece. But scattered far and wide? Hardly!

Moreover, for the wreckage to be noticeable when spread
over such a wide area, it would have to have come from something far larger than any common weather balloon and reflector. Pieces of one of those couldn't possibly have produced the
strong reaction from rancher Brazel. A few newly emptied beer
bottles would have made a greater impression.

And there's the matter of the original conclusion that it was a
"genuine flying disc" versus the later "balloon" explanation.
Sheep rancher Brazel may have led a life of isolation, without
even a telephone, but that doesn't mean he was naive or stupid.
To survive, let alone prosper, in the ranching business in the
1940s demanded a degree of astuteness that would have canceled out any realistic possibility that Brazel would have gotten
all worked up over something as ordinary as a weather balloon.

Like most rural Westerners, he knew what a weather balloon looked like, having picked up more than one and turned it in for the small reward, as per a notice listed on the device.

Then, when the disc/balloon remains were first seen by military people, how could the "misidentification" have been compounded? Could the intelligence officer of one of the Army Air Forces' elite units have been so foolish as to fail to recognize a common balloon? Maj. Jesse Marcel didn't hold his prestigious, responsible position because he was some senator's son-in-law. He was the intelligence officer of the world's only atomic bombing outfit because he knew how to deal with difficult situations and with unexpected events without jumping to baseless and thus potentially dangerous conclusions.

Brazel and Marcel knew that what they had seen wasn't even a distant relative of a weather balloon, or anything else familiar. But they were effectively silenced, as were all the others who could have let the cat out of the bag. Many of the military people saw enough of the recovered wreckage and bodies to realize that something terribly important was going on. It appears that those who were not needed for the analysis of the materials and bodies were shipped out to separate bases many thousands of miles away, where there would be no one to talk to about crashed flying saucers. At least, no one who could be counted on not to laugh. Those who had to be entrusted with sensitive details of the shocking secret were those who could be trusted to keep their mouths shut.

The two groups that might have gotten wind of the true story and learned enough about it to pose a threat to government secrecy were the press and the scientific community. Their cooperation—conscious or not, voluntary or otherwise—would have been absolutely vital if the bizarre nature of UFOs was to be kept secret from the American people.

If the press began paying undue attention to reports of UFO sightings, that would lead to more published reports and to more widespread serious interest and then to a loss of confidence in the government's handling (or apparent mishandling) of the situation. Only if the great majority of members of the press (and through them, of course, the public) believed the government's lame explanations for UFO sightings, would it remain possible for knowledge of the importance of UFOs to be held in check. It would take only one or two leading columnists or commentators to wreck the structure being built to contain the UFO mystery.

The scientific community, like the press, played a much bigger role in this than anyone could have realized at the time. As long as there wasn't a single important spokesman for science displaying any enthusiasm for UFO reality, it would be easy for the government to support its position that UFOs amounted to nothing that would interest intelligent people. But if even one major scientist was willing to speak out in favor of the serious study of UFOs (apart from whatever was being done by the military behind closed doors) the ability to maintain an atmosphere of foolishness would be in great danger.

The press cooperated, though almost certainly without realizing it was doing so. It ridiculed flying saucers and implied that those who thought they were anything more than hallucinations or mistakes were simply not worth paying any attention to. This fed upon itself, so that no newsman wanted to risk ridicule from his fellow newsmen by showing interest in the subject. And it was subtly fed by the government with a stream of summary reports, statistics, and blanket denials, all of which stressed the total lack of substance to UFO reports. With the government saying it was a lot of fuss about nothing, and no reliable source providing contradictory information, what was a reporter to do but go along with the official line?

The scientific community cooperated just as fully, and probably was no more aware of its complicity than was the press. Here, as well, the government was faced with the dual challenges of the scientist's avowed intellectual and moral obligations to uncover the truth. To reduce the chances that scientists would embark on their own UFO investigations and perhaps learn more than the government thought was advisable, the services of one of their own were enlisted. Dr. Donald Menzel, respected veteran of Harvard's observatory and Astronomy Department, wrote a book in 1953—*Flying Saucers*—in which he sneered at the idea that even a single UFO sighting might amount to more than pathetic incompetence on the part of some grossly unqualified or overly emotional layman. He "knew" that no true scientist would think he had seen a genuine flying saucer; after all, he had been able to explain those he had seen.

Despite the fact that the late Dr. Menzel used some amazing distortions of science to make his point (such as that alternating layers of hot and cold air can act like "air lenses" and bend light rays so much that lights on the ground will appear to be overhead), not one noted scientist was willing to challenge him until Dr. James McDonald, University of Arizona atmospheric physicist, spoke up in the 1960s and was roundly ridiculed. The fear of being grouped with "amateur UFO experts" in opposition to the vast majority of scientists, was too great to be overcome by any need to be objective.

For decades, every well-publicized UFO report was met by at least one scientist willing to go on record explaining the event as nothing more substantive than a mirage, or a swarm of electrified insects, or energy released by a minor earth tremor. It didn't seem to matter that the explanation failed to fit what was described by the observer, or that the explanation might involve previously unknown and unverified scientific principles or phenomena. All that counted was that a genuine scientist had easily explained what a rank amateur had thought was unexplainable.

The press, not to be outdone by the scientific community, stressed explanation over data. So what if a solid, respectable citizen claimed to have been terrified by some hovering, disc-shaped craft that shone a bright light into his car and lit its interior? If some scientist (whose background may have been far removed from meteoritics) said it must have been a meteor, then it must have been a meteor. Overlooked in the rush to find an answer was the fact that a meteor cannot hover, nor can it shine a beam of light anywhere.

The government didn't have to go out of its way to pressure

or even influence the press and scientists as long as their own were willing to do the government's work for it. And they were encouraged in their misguided efforts by the lunatic fringe of the private UFO community. Even the most open-minded reporter was left quivering in fear for his reputation when assailed by some wild-eyed flying saucer evangelist insisting that even the least believable of UFO reports was "proof" that the aliens are here, and that at least one of them has been beaming messages of truth and beauty into his head.

With scientists and reporters thus firmly in the government camp even if they didn't realize it, there were but two factions which possessed the potential for upsetting the status quo: private UFO investigators and those who operated the UFOs.

Serious private investigators, even when grouped into associations, generally have been unable to make effective use of the often impressive evidence and analyses they have produced. If most scientists won't back them up (or even pay them any attention) and the press won't take them seriously, how can they get their messages out?

When a serious-minded private UFO group starts to capture the attention of the press, it can pose a significant threat to the official secrecy policy. In the mid-1960s, the National Investigations Committee on Aerial Phenomena (NICAP) acquired considerable influence with the Washington press corps, often getting quoted ahead of official spokesmen. It was thus able to make the nation aware of some of the more glaring weaknesses in the government's handling of the UFO problem. But when the air force closed down its Project Blue Book in 1969, public interest and support dried up, and NICAP faded away.

Despite the steady stream of detailed reports of close-up observations of radical craft having performance far beyond anything known or even theorized, there was no demand for a more objective look at UFOs from either journalists or scientists. The occasional faint call for a rethinking of the UFO evidence was overwhelmed by sarcastic denunciations from self-appointed protectors of scientific purity and by the ridiculous headlines in the supermarket tabloids.

The only other group that seems to stand much of a chance of effecting changes in the status quo is the UFO operators, be they aliens or Albanians. If they decide to alter their behavior and become more open—perhaps landing and presenting themselves for the TV cameras, or at least to the crowd at a softball game—all the rules will change instantly. So far, however, their behavior can best be described as furtive, with little evidence that they want to be seen, let alone meet humans on anything like even terms.

It wasn't that there wasn't a single scientist or reporter interested in the UFO mystery; a lot of them had admitted to long-term interest, in private. Rather, it was that hardly any was willing to speak out in the face of general apathy and peer disapproval. There were increasing signs of fear in these two groups of people who were otherwise seen as courageous and far-sighted. They feared not physical harm, but professional and intellectual harm that could result from an open show of interest, let alone of support for UFO reality.

A columnist for a major daily newspaper told one of the authors that he thought the story might actually be "too big"! This previously unknown journalistic concept was explained as the result of the probable chain of reasoning that would follow any serious investigation of UFOs. To wit, a reporter who took a close look at the evidence might well conclude that UFOs could be alien craft. This would inevitably lead to consideration of the staggering political, economic, and cultural ramifications of contact with another intelligent life-form. This in turn could lead the reporter to reject his other professional responsibilities as suddenly inconsequential and focus on UFOs to the exclusion of all else. His effectiveness as a reporter would suffer and he could lose his job. It wouldn't be worth the trouble.

By establishing a sham official investigation—Projects Sign, Grudge, and Blue Book—the government was able to convince enough people that it was dealing conscientiously with the problem. Not until the files of Project Blue Book, et al became available long after its demise could it be seen that, far from being a scientific investigation, it was phony. But for more than two decades it was used to portray the government as taking the mystery seriously and finding nothing to support the idea that UFOs are real and unexplained.

The government's insistence that it had closed its doors on UFOs in December, 1969 was seen by science and the press as proof that the subject had little basis in fact. After twenty-two years of fighting off attacks based on the demonstrated ineptitude of its official, public investigation, the government discovered in 1969 that silence is a good defense. Faced with documentary evidence that, for instance, Project Blue Book never received reports having national security implications and that such reports would continue to be handled through intelligence procedures set up for the purpose, the air force continues to issue its stock denial of both interest and involvement. The CIA, despite the existence in private hands of its own documents that show interest well into the 1970s, insists it has had no interest in UFOs since 1953.

13

After the Crash

ONCE THE U.S. government realized how important and sensitive the debris from the crashes were, it began a new and much more vital phase of the operation. For reasons that can be surmised if not proved, all releases of news were stopped, and all testimony and evidence that might conflict with the official line (that it was no more than a weather balloon) were sealed off from the public.

The first two USAAF men to become aware of the radical nature of some of the crash wreckage—Major Marcel and Captain Cavitt—were officially and legally silenced. Mac Brazel, who found the material, was taken into custody on some national-security pretense and during several days with the military was convinced that it would be in his and the country's best interests if he would change his story to coincide with the official position. Brazel went to his grave without ever speaking out to the contrary.

To make certain that no one beyond the government's legal control got his or her hands on any of the wreckage (which would have proved that the recovered object was not a balloon and that the government was lying), a team went out from Roswell AAF to the Foster ranch site, and from Kirtland AAF or Alamogordo AAF or Sandia to the Plains of San Agustin, to pick up every little scrap. As an indication of the extreme importance placed on this, several weeks later, a casual remark by Mac Brazel's son, Bill, to the effect that he had collected a few bits of wreckage, quickly led to a visit by official persons who confiscated it.

The intensive searches of the crash site near Corona almost certainly coincided with the expanded search of the surrounding area for the remainder of the craft, since it was obvious that the material found on the sheep ranch could not have been the entire vehicle. A day or two after the start of the major recovery effort, and almost a week after the crash at the ranch, the rest of the craft was located several miles from where the original debris had been found. At about the same time, three (or possibly four) bodies were found in what was assumed to be escape capsules, within a mile or two of the main body of the craft. This discovery was probably made from the air, by airplanes or helicopters from Roswell AAF or some nearby base such as Alamogordo.

Once trucks had brought back as much of the wreckage as they could carry to Roswell AAF, it had to be stored in a large, secure building, where it was guarded carefully while trusted men inside packed it for shipment to locations where it could be calmly studied, tested, and analyzed. The bodies had to be preserved against further deterioration, using whatever techniques could be adapted from contemporary embalming practice.

The limited amount of wreckage brought back from the ranch to Roswell AAF by Marcel and Cavitt was loaded into the bomb bay of a B-29 bomber and flown to Fort Worth, where General Ramey took over the operation, clamping down on all talk and replacing reality with the tale of the weather balloon. It is assumed that some or all of the material was quickly flown on to Wright Field, because of the testimony of several aircrew members and a July 8, 1947, FBI teletype message stating "disc and balloon being transported to Wright Field by special plane for examination." The limited ability of a B-29 to carry a large volume of cargo would restrict its usefulness as an impromptu freighter.

Just how many airplanes were used to ship all the material

recovered from the Corona crash sites is not known, though scraps of testimony suggest one more B-29 and three Douglas C-54 Skytrooper four-engined transports were used, along with as many as three B-25 Mitchell twin-engined medium bombers that may have carried bodies to different locations.

How the main part of the craft was dealt with at either site is unknown. If it was too large to be transported by standard army trucks, as seems the case, special equipment must have been brought in, as it is doubtful that it could have been dismantled and loaded into or onto small vehicles. Since heavy-lift helicopters did not exist in 1947, the main part of the craft would have had to come out by land, over poor-to-nonexistent roads. But as hardly anyone lived in that part of New Mexico, the chances of identifiable wreckage being seen were minimal, especially if the removal were conducted at night.

In view of the highly consistent descriptions of the debris found at the Foster ranch site, it is apparent that all of the material was exceptionally unusual: very strong, very light, and very different from anything previously seen. Analysis of such material would require the best brains and the finest equipment that could be obtained at Wright Field and other military installations, along with the nation's universities and industry.

A man such as Dr. Vannevar Bush would have been needed to get through to the top people in the appropriate scientific and engineering disciplines. He would have had the prestige necessary to get them to participate in this novel task without their first asking a lot of questions he could not risk answering over the telephone.

The amazing strength of the materials could have posed serious and fascinating problems when it came to conducting conventional tests. It may not have been possible to perform the sort of experiments scientists traditionally use, such as testing the shear strength by cutting, the tensile strength by pulling, and the compression strength by crushing. The foil, I beams, and "parchment" could easily have withstood the best efforts to slice, poke, twist, stretch, and squash.

Unless parts of the craft were designed to be dismantled easily (that is, were attached with something like screws or bolts), scientists and technicians could have spent weeks, months, or even years just trying to reduce it to manageable proportions. One result could well have been the development of new methods for scientific testing, as the intellectual challenge posed by such totally unexpected materials could have motivated men to become highly creative. They could just as easily have produced some nervous breakdowns.

Small elements of equipment that may have been found in the main part of the craft could have offered simpler challenges. Devices meant for extravehicular use were therefore intentionally removable, such as life-support equipment or sample-collection containers, might have revealed their purposes and even functions with the simple depression of a button or flick of a switch. Or by the activation of unsuspected triggers purely by chance.

If the craft had anything like an airplane or spacecraft instrument panel, it may have been possible to remove one or more "instruments" and, by attaching a power supply and measuring devices, to learn something about how they worked. It is just as possible that, for example, systems used for indicating performance may have been completely baffling, suggesting no obvious ways of operation and understanding.

It is probable that as the months wore on with something less than total mastery of this alien technology, more and more specialists would have been called in, and the total number of people aware of at least part of the nature of the matter would have grown considerably. The difficulty of maintaining absolute secrecy would thus have been increased, and so would the need for effective long-term techniques for controlling all possible leaks of information.

It is quite possible that a special laboratory was established to deal with the remains of the crash and the bodies, or even several laboratories in different parts of the country that may have specialized in work on materials, equipment, language, and so on. There is some reason to believe that one of these may have been at Kirtland AFB, near Albuquerque, New Mexico,

operated by the U.S. Navy which may have had specially qualified people needed for such an investigation, or may simply
have insisted on being a part of a uniquely important, interesting, and prestigious project.

The bodies, according to the testimony of people who were
directly aware of them, would probably have been more sus-
ceptible to conventional analytical techniques. Medical people familiar with autopsies should have been able to do the
preliminary work, since there is no indication that the bodies
were so different as to baffle doctors. A scalpel may be just as
effective in dividing an alien corpse into small pieces as it is
on humans. Other common medical procedures, such as
studying biopsies under high magnification, may have produced considerable information, if not knowledge or understanding.

Security precautions surrounding the temporary or permanent storage of bodies would have had to be even more strin-
gent than those for the wreckage, as the alien nature of the
bodies would be apparent at a glance to even an untrained eye.
Moreover, the matter of the strange and powerful smell of the
bodies adds to the difficulty of keeping the whole thing secret.
There is at least one report of widespread interest being
aroused at Wright-Patterson by a most peculiar odor detected
by employees in a neighboring lab not involved in the alien
study. The initial admission of the nature of the smell was
quickly retracted and the trail almost obliterated.

The ability of the U.S. government to clamp down on all
knowledge and discussion of a crash was not as well developed
in 1947 as it obviously has become since then. It appears that
the army learned of the crash at Foster Ranch several days after
the fact, and then only because a civilian voluntarily showed
some pieces to a sheriff. By the time the lid was slammed down,
a lot of people had seen and handled bits of the wreckage, and
others were aware of its nature. Since then, techniques for
controlling such situations have obviously been refined, for
none of the subsequent rumored crashes has been testified to in
anything but the vaguest way.

The effectiveness of the government's long-term control of

all knowledge surrounding the New Mexico crashes has been nothing short of outstanding, though of questionable morality. For several decades, the crash was seen as a misidentification of no real importance. The radar-reflector cover story was accepted without question or exception by the press, and by the time a private UFO community emerged, the trail was so cold and faint that no one bothered to try to follow it.

The concealment of the research into the nature of the recovered wreckage and bodies was equally superb, as was the hiding of the great extent of the hardware that must have resulted from as few as two or as many as a half-dozen crashes. And the mountain of paperwork that must have been generated by the recovery, transportation, study, analysis, and concealment of the material and bodies was also adeptly handled.

Once the U.S. government had its hands on enough wreckage and bodies to convince its leaders that it was dealing with an alien civilization that was, in some ways, far ahead of our own, it had no choice but to organize an unprecedented effort to learn everything possible about this new force in our society.

First, the remains would have to be studied by the best brains available, within the limitations of extreme security. Only scientists who were willing to keep their involvement totally secret could possibly be trusted with such volatile information. The dangers inherent in even the smallest leak of information were so great that total trustworthiness had to have been at least as important as the most awesome of scientific qualifications.

STUDYING THE REMAINS

Once the collected wreckage, bodies, living beings, reports, photographs, and other evidence of a crash had been delivered by a combination of government air and ground vehicles to one or more secret "alien material research centers" or specialized departments within publicly known government or private facilities, the work of analysis could begin. At first, this must have been a relatively crude process, as there had been no prior events to prepare the analysts for such a novel experience. But as knowledge was gained from the remains of a first crash, methods and increasingly elaborate and sophisticated procedures must have been devised and refined by the most talented and creative people available.

On the assumption that no English-language "owner's manual" was found in New Mexico in 1947, the analysts would have had to poke and prod and wiggle and twist and lift and thump every piece of the wreckage, before and after efforts to reassemble the craft in much the same way that airplane-accident investigators attempt to put a wrecked airplane back together from the broken bits found at its crash site.

Study of the wreckage and bodies would have to be divided into logical subdivisions, with experts developing as knowledge was acquired:

DESIGN OF THE CRAFT:

External design, internal design, construction, propulsion, flight controls, navigation, communication, life support, crew facilities, extravehicular devices, stealth technology, maintenance and repair, the occupants.

DETECTION AND LOCATION OF CRASHES:

The *"crash/retrieval team"*: wreckage acquisition, recording of data, security, packing and removing the remains, team composition.

ATTEMPTING TO COMMUNICATE

Armed with the knowledge that there was at least one intelligent species out there in space, the government had to be terribly eager to establish communication in hopes of learning what the wreckage and bodies could not possibly reveal: who the aliens are, where they come from, why they are here, do they plan to harm us, will they teach us what they know?

But how do you communicate with those about whom you know so little? How do you send someone an invitation to a scientific symposium or even a ballgame when you don't know their address? How do you ask them even the most basic of questions when you don't know their language, or even if they use language? How do you exchange ideas if you haven't a clue about how their minds work? Or even, by our standards, if they communicate at all?

Those who had gotten closest to living aliens in the early part of the 1947 wave of flying saucer sightings were pilots whose airplanes had been buzzed or paced in flight. For a pilot, the simplest form of communication—and the most familiar—is rocking his wings. It says "Hello, do you see me?" The nighttime counterpart of this is flashing one's landing lights and looking for a similar signal in return. Neither of these techniques involves the transfer of much information but is merely a friendly acknowledgement.

There have been many reports of pilots, motorists, and even campers with flashlights who have gotten a response from UFOs, but never of an organized scientific effort to say "Hi, there! We know you're there and want to get to know you!" Still, the need to communicate must have been so great that the silliest of schemes would be preferable to none at all.

Probably the first attempts at communication were spontaneous, by pilots rocking their wings, flashing their lights, and even trying to call the UFO crew by radio. While radio certainly offers the opportunity to say much more than simply "Howdy!," it involves transmission and reception frequencies and, more important, language. But the technique was so simple and so obvious that its naivete must be excused.

Of course, if radio contact was established with the UFOs on the first attempts, then all bets are off. We have no clue about what was communicated, and thus what the impact was, if any. But on the assumption that more sophisticated techniques were required, we can make an educated guess as to what might then have been tried.

Since most of the better-publicized sightings early in the

1947 wave were made in the Pacific Northwest, the government may have hurriedly set up high-powered radio transmitters and sensitive receivers in Washington and Oregon to try to call the aliens and listen for their transmissions to us and to each other. But the 1947 wave soon spread out to cover the entire United States, and so the chances of achieving short-range communication from any one location were pretty small.

Still, something had to be done, and done quickly before some "amateur" called them and got a meaningful answer which he then passed along to the press. Since we knew nothing about the aliens' methods of communicating, we had to try anything that was suggested, which is a very inefficient way to operate, and probably didn't impress those we hoped would be on the other end of the line.

It had to be faced that we were—and may still be—operating from a position of gross ignorance. We didn't know how to communicate or if the aliens had any interest in hearing from us. They might have seen us as no more than the equivalent of white rats in a laboratory: What medical researcher spends much time wondering if the rats are trying to communicate with him? Or it could have been that the vast differences in culture and biology could make communication all but impossible even if the attempt were being made, as it has long been with dolphins.

But the attempt had to be made, for the potential gain to mankind (to say nothing of the honors that would be heaped upon the first person to talk with an alien) would be so great that to ignore the possibility would be unthinkable. If the aliens use a means of communication that we would consider language, then some really clever people just might be able to manage an elementary translation of a message.

But what if they communicate with thoughts rather than words? Or in some manner that no human has ever considered? Then the chances of getting through to them would depend almost entirely on their willingness and ability to get through to us. Their appearance in our skies would probably have been the result of some long-range planning, and so they may have given more thought to communication than we, who had suddenly become aware of their presence with little advance warning.

Another possible means of communication that could have been arranged on short notice would be some visual signals, such as a large picture laid out on the ground showing a human offering a bouquet of flowers to our visitors. This assumes, of course, that our cultural behavior would mean about the same to them as it does to us, rather than the opposite or nothing at all. Do you see the problem? Those faced with the challenge of trying to "talk" to the aliens wouldn't have the slightest idea what they were doing!

But we would have to try, or miss a historic opportunity. One clue could be found on the I beams recovered at Foster Ranch, to say nothing of what may have been found in the main part of that craft or the one that crashed at the Plains of San Agustin. Armed with what had to be considered alien writing (but could have been something else), we would have put our top linguists to work and could have learned something. At least enough to make our communication attempts a little more than shots in the dark.

Whether any attempts to establish an exchange were made is, of course, secret, as are any results.

14

The Crash Site Today

YOU CAN TALK to ten witnesses to the New Mexico crashes, or to twenty-five. It's all the same: They were there and you weren't. When it happened you were a kid, and less able to see through the official blanket of secrecy and deception than most. Now, you have to deal with possibly the most important event in history as an outsider. No matter how familiar you become with the details, your information is, at best, secondhand.

But there is one way to get close to what happened: Travel to the crash sites and have a look for yourself. You can pretend to look for remnants of the two vehicles that slammed into the ranches, and you can dream of the impact you could have on world history if only you can find even a little piece. But really what you are doing is trying to get in touch with those long-gone days. This is stable country where little changes from decade to decade. Not like big cities where twenty-five-year-old buildings are torn down to make way for newer ones. New Mexico hangs on to its proud past; New Mexico is pretty much the same.

And most of New Mexico is almost empty. Travel more than a few miles from the fully modern city of Albuquerque and you find yourself in open country that probably looks about the way it did a century ago. Oh, sure, there are TV satellite dishes and some shiny new American cars. But the hills and the valleys and the mountains and the dried-up river beds and the scrubby little trees are the same as greeted the pioneers. Once off the well-kept paved roads and onto dirt and gravel, you have no trouble visualizing the enormous cattle drives that once formed the basis for the New Mexico economy and the background for a few hundred Western movies.

Visualizing what happened in July 1947 is a lot harder. One of the most important events in history has left no trace on the land, and precious few details in the minds of New Mexicans. The land was scoured of every bit of wreckage of the 1947 crashes, and the memories of most of those who were involved have been effectively contained behind a wall of official secrecy. The justification is national security, though "national insecurity" may be closer to the truth.

The route to the Corona site begins along paved roads where sheep graze just off the shoulder, staring with intense curiosity as strangers motor past and then returning to their never-ending search for nourishment in the sparse grasses. It's then onto rough dirt roads offering fascinating views of the land and an occasional building, but few familiar signs of civilization. Finally a teeth-rattling drive on a crude path that could easily be mistaken for an accident of nature, except that it heads off from the single landmark you've been given.

The site itself hardly looks like the place an alien spacecraft once spewed its parts following what must have been a catastrophic accident. It looks like a thousand other places in central New Mexico: gently rolling hills dotted with tough little trees and bushes. The grass, thanks to no more than a few inches of rain each year, doesn't look like it could support much life, yet this is cattle country, and cows and sheep do eke out a living from it.

In 1947, the scattered trees and bushes and grass were pretty much like they are today. Only they had company. One part of this inhospitable land was peppered with pieces of strange material, another part played host to a craft from another world, and still a third was the almost-final resting place for several voyagers from afar. It's probably not the place they expected to end their days.

Today it takes an active imagination to picture that time in the hot summer of 1947 when something went terribly wrong. Just why a vehicle capable of traveling uncountable millions of miles was unable to cope with something it experienced in New Mexico's sky remains unknown, at least outside the Pentagon. But something totally unexpected happened, and the world changed in secret.

As much as fifty acres was covered with mostly small pieces of odd metallic foil, slim I beams, heavy paper, and black plastic. Cattle and horses reportedly shied away from it, preferring to walk around the debris. Something told them it wasn't anything normal. Priorities changed overnight. No longer was the feeding and watering of sheep the primary concern, for there had been an intrusion into the tough, securely routine life of the sheep rancher.

Many hours of dedicated searching for even the smallest scrap of material left over from the trauma of 1947 have turned up nothing at all. Hundreds of rocks have been turned over, revealing nothing but the occasional little scorpion. Bushes that look like they date back to the last ice age have been poked and prodded and had their roots scraped clean of dirt. Still, nothing to raise an eyebrow.

How could a crew of GIs, few of whom had any experience in country as wild as this, do such a thorough job of collecting all the pieces of an unknown vehicle? No one knew what it looked like before it broke up, and so no one could estimate how much material should be in the field. And yet all of it apparently was collected and returned to Roswell AAF to be crated up, loaded into C-54s, and flown out to where scientists must have been shivering in anticipation.

The big pieces would have been obvious, and a careful search would have turned up smaller ones. But what if the debris had included some very small bits that neither reflected sunlight nor responded to metal detectors? Shouldn't there still be some of them in hiding? Somewhere downstream of the main debris area, where the occasional rains may have washed them? Or where the frequently strong winds could have blown them?

It seems reasonable, but as yet not a single tiny scrap has been found. And while almost a half-century has passed, the urge to have one more look cannot be resisted. You walk slowly, cautiously over the rough ground, your eyes focused just in front of your feet. Kick a clump of dirt, push back a gnarled old limb, pry apart a recently split rock. No matter how preposterous the odds, it must be done, for the joy on finding a piece of spacecraft must instantly blot out the growing feeling of embarrassment at spending so much time on such an obviously hopeless task.

You tell yourself there's hardly a chance in a million of finding anything. Yet one chance in a million is infinitely better than no chances. It means that it's possible you'll find what others have failed to find. A scrap of stuff that will briefly lift you off this battered old planet on a flight to the one from which the craft came so many years ago. But it is a flight of fancy. There's nothing here but common shrubs and trees and grass and dirt and rocks.

And yet . . . you have to keep going. Who knows but what the very next rock will reveal a piece of silvery foil that has been waiting almost two generations for you. It's hot and lonely and the thin air is uncomfortably dry. It's a strange place for city folk, but it must have been a far stranger place for the visitors who ended their days here. No matter why they were flying over New Mexico, they died here, and so perhaps this place should be given greater respect. When astronauts or cosmonauts finally visit another inhabited world and perhaps die in the effort, how will we feel about the locals tramping around that crash site in hopes of finding souvenirs?

The longer you poke around the dusty hills of the sheep ranch and find nothing, the more you feel like quitting. No, not exactly like quitting, but more like postponing the final and possibly successful attack on a bunch of innocent rocks and bushes that must be hiding the high-tech Grail. Convinced there is something to be found, you have temporarily run out of patience and need to move on.

Back you go across the crudest roads you have ever seen, to what passes as a highway in these parts, and thence to the glorified crossroads called Corona. After a day in some truly desolate places, this seems like civilization. It's a pleasure to finally get out of first gear! And head westward to the Plains of San Agustin, where far fewer UFO investigators have preceded you. More cows, maybe, but they were looking for tasteless stuff to chew, not to make history.

A hundred fifty miles later, you come upon the stark one-time great lake, and soon the eerie and deceptively large saucer-shaped electronic antennas. The Very Large Array stretches across the highway, its thirteen-mile long arms spread out to capture radio signals so faint that only a scientist can appreciate the achievement. This part of Catron County—the least populated in the state—was chosen for the world's largest radio telescope because it is electronically quiet, without the interfering signals to be found elsewhere. Not because it is near the site of the crash of a strange vehicle, as some overly dramatic saucer fans have suggested.

Past the VLA you drive, wondering what it's looking at today. Off to the left stretches the Plains, long-ago home to Anastazis and Athabascans and other ancient peoples whose descendants can be found driving pick-up trucks past the VLA with rarely a glance at the familiar formation of slowly moving monuments.

The flatness of the Plains contrasts sharply with the surrounding steep, rocky hills and you can't help but wonder if the crew that was about to crash might have been looking for a level landing field. But there's no way to know what they were thinking, or how desperate was their situation just before they hit the ground. Still, you have to try to understand what might have been happening, even if you know you can't possibly come to a meaningful conclusion.

You're driving along a good road, but there is hardly any traffic and there's no surplus of tourist facilities. The sleepy little town of Magdalena has one diner and a couple of motels, none of which looks particularly appetizing. You go on to Datil (rhymes with *cattle*) and the Eagle Guest Ranch, which doesn't look like much at first glance, either, but turns out to be a comfortable, friendly motel/restaurant/general store that serves as a sort of community center. You get the feeling that everyone within twenty-five miles or more will stop in to get caught up on the local news.

The crash site is a good drive from here, at the edge of a large cattle ranch. It offers a few more trees than there were at Corona, but the grass and bushes look the same. Lots of rocks, too. And not a single trace of the crash that reportedly killed three aliens and left one alive, though perhaps wishing he weren't. Again, you walk around as slowly and methodically as you can, staring at the ground and trying to will a piece or two of wreckage into existence.

There isn't any more of it to be found here than there was at the sheep ranch. But you keep looking, afraid that if you stop, the very next rock you might otherwise have turned over will continue to hide its extraterrestrial treasure. After a couple of hours you tell yourself that you have to face up to reality. This could go on forever, and since you don't have that kind of time, you cancel plans to inspect every square inch of an area that has no specific boundaries.

So far, your trip has turned up nothing to justify the time and expense. You've seen deer and antelope and even a couple of elk. But you can see those in any zoo, along with considerably more exotic creatures. Pieces of 1947-vintage wreckage, if they are even within miles of here, remain tantalizingly beyond reach. Was this journey really to find absolute, physical proof of the crash of an alien spacecraft, or merely to show off your determination? The search had to be made, but its motivations are far from clear.

You take one final glance around the totally natural collection of rocks and flora (including some startlingly colorful flowers barely large enough to survive) and then you pack it in. If there is anything left here that arrived in a blaze of mystery, it will have to wait for a more intensive search. You hate to admit it, but you're bored. Bored from looking for scraps of unknown material that came from an unknown place, for an unknown reason. The words suggest a terribly special kind of excitement, but your feet are tired and your eyes are tired and all you have to show for your hard work is shoes full of dust.

Can it be that the government got everything? Years of dealing with a host of official agencies and bureaus and offices have left you with the strong sense that 100 percent efficiency is as rare as . . . pieces of spaceships. There have to be at least one or two scraps that aren't locked in vaults. After all, Pappy Henderson, who flew one of the transports loaded with boxed wreckage, managed to pocket a piece, as did at least one of the sergeants who helped box it. How about all of the GIs who scoured the crash sites? Did they all resist the wonderful temptation?

Some place out there is a whole collection of pieces. In an old coffee can, or a cigar box, or in that battered old trunk up in the attic where Grandpa's army uniform rests, along with the neatly folded flag that briefly covered his coffin. A piece of the foil could easily have been slipped between the pages of a book. For that matter, some pieces could be sitting on someone's mantel, their origin completely unsuspected.

15

Implications

THE SHORT-TERM and long-term implications of something as complex, unusual, and controversial as the recovery of crashed alien vehicles would be difficult to determine even if all the facts were known and public. But when the very nature of the events is vehemently denied by the government, few qualified individuals are willing to put their wisdom and expertise to work on the problem.

Because they look at the situation so differently, the two authors have decided to approach this aspect of the situation separately. But while they see the implications in their own ways, that does not mean they disagree on the basic elements of the impact of the 1947 crashes. The views of Don Berliner will be followed by those of Stanton Friedman.

When an oak tree standing alone in an empty field is struck by lightning, the impact of the event is limited to that single tree. Even if it is shattered and killed, not one other tree, no human, and at most a few squirrels are affected. The immediate and the long-term impacts are the same. The loss is routine and easily accepted.

But when the first UFO crashed in New Mexico in July 1947, all that kept the long-term impact from being as great as that of any event in recorded history was the U.S. government's preventing the world from knowing what happened. It was anything but routine and acceptable, at least to the select few who were permitted to learn about it.

Mankind's position at the very top of the evolutionary ladder, considered a source of immense pride for eons, was suddenly placed in serious jeopardy. The absolute ruler of all the Earth (and presumably everywhere else, too) was on the verge of being revealed as inferior in some respects to those about whom he knew nothing and of whose very existence he was uncertain.

Someone had been flying through Man's private skies in vehicles vastly superior to anything developed here on Earth. And even though at least one of them had crashed, they were clearly the product of a civilization having far greater knowledge of science and technology. Man might still claim to be the master of the Earth, but suddenly there was proof that someone else was smarter, had started sooner, or had progressed faster. Man might still be able to divert great rivers, clear vast forests, tame wild horses, and teach puppydogs to sit up. But the designers, builders, and pilots of the UFOs had awe-inspiring knowledge (if not necessarily wisdom) and could well be in position to submit Man to their own will.

Within two weeks of the start of the first great American wave of UFO sightings in 1947, it had become obvious that the strange craft were far faster and more maneuverable than any known flying machines. Moreover, they could fly almost silently and seemed capable of controlling their radar profile. Any realistic chance that they might be the tools of some other country was wiped out by the discovery of the remains of two crashed examples in the wilds of New Mexico. The mere presence of superlight, superstrong materials of unknown composition should have been enough to indicate their alien nature. But the discovery of several small nonhumans in the wreckage eliminated the last hope that Man might still deserve credit for this enormous leap forward.

By keeping all knowledge of this amazing discovery secret the U.S. government postponed the day when Man would realize that his place in the cosmos was not quite as lofty as he thought. By restricting knowledge of the aliens' activities to the government's chosen advisers and thus losing potentially priceless advice from knowledgeable outsiders, it slowed the process of learning about the aliens and working out ways to deal with their presence. It also put off the day of reckoning, when our government would finally be called to task for its peculiar behavior.

Of course, the government may have had good reasons for keeping the initial news of the discovery of aliens secret . . . or at least it may have thought it had good reasons. At first, it feared the "flying discs" might be some terribly advanced form of Soviet aircraft or missiles developed by captured Nazi scientists. In the early postwar period, nothing would have been more frightening than the prospect of the overflight of advanced Soviet weapons, and so the eagerness to keep the facts quiet was understandable. At least until it became obvious that the mysterious flying things were just too far advanced to be the result of any Soviet-Nazi collaboration. Since we knew they weren't ours, and no other nation on Earth could have made the required technical progress, the possibility of their being alien had to be faced.

But until we knew for certain who was responsible for the flying discs and that they were not a threat to national security, it must have seemed prudent to remain silent. The discovery of proof of the discs' alien nature answered one of the big questions, but there still remained the possibility that they were unfriendly. Their failure to zap anyone with Buck Rogers-style ray guns might be evidence of subtlety, rather than friendliness.

Despite the brilliantly effective security system imposed by the U.S. government, the facts of the flying discs appearance and behavior could not be hidden forever, as they were being seen and reported publicly by thousands of people, among whom were scores of professional pilots, scientists, engineers, and others whose knowledge and skill made their reports believable despite the bizarre content. The descriptions were sufficiently consistent to point to a novel class of flying machines bearing no similarity to anything created by any known government.

The realization that these UFOs were quite possibly alien vehicles gradually made its way into the public consciousness despite the best efforts of government disinformation specialists, the self-appointed protectors of scientific conservatism, and the damage to credibility caused by UFO reports in the supermarket tabloid newspapers and from the lunatic fringe of the private UFO community. Lacking any other explanation for the most baffling UFO reports, more and more people assumed they were alien in origin, even though they knew of no direct evidence of this.

As for the aliens' motives, they were a lot harder to understand. Most people figured they were exploring Earth and its people for reasons of scientific curiosity, because that is what we plan to do when we get to other planets. Their continued presence in large numbers for at least several decades suggests, however, that if they are explorers, they may be slow learners, or we may be particularly hard to figure out (which would give Man at least a temporary boost in self-esteem). But for most of the modern era of UFOs, no other motivation on the part of the UFO operators was given serious consideration.

Until 1981, when New York author Budd Hopkins began to take a close look at the strangest of all the parts of the UFO mystery: so-called alien abductions. These short-term kidnappings of people by apparent aliens, most of which involve puzzling procedures resembling medical examinations, first became public in the mid-1960s with the publication of *The Interrupted Journey* by John Fuller. He described the extraordinary experiences of Barney and Betty Hill, whose return from an otherwise normal vacation included a side trip into history. In the following decade, a few similar stories came to light, but generally remained within the UFO community.

Hopkins' *Missing Time* and *Intruders* sold widely, and firmly established alien abductions as a subject for talk shows and their vast TV audiences. The books described dozens of "abduction" reports that Hopkins had investigated and brought thousands of letters from suspected "abductees" to him and then to best-selling novelist Whitley Strieber, whose *Communion* (about his personal abductionlike experiences) was read by millions. The amazing consistency of now many hundreds of individual accounts, and the inability of mental health professionals to find an alternative explanation for the emotion-packed symptoms, strongly suggest these unfortunate people are the victims of some very strange phenomenon.

It is the contention of Hopkins and other serious investigators that the "aliens" are conducting genetic experiments on thousands of innocent people—often over several generations—and even using them to produce hybrid offspring. The researchers freely admit this sounds outlandish but insist the evidence supports it.

If this is the case, and there is some reason to believe the U.S. government is aware of it, then its reluctance to open its most secret UFO files becomes more understandable. The government is charged with the responsibility of protecting the public from foreign threats, and any admission that aliens are having their way with hundreds of Americans could well lead to political disruption.

Just picture yourself seated at the great desk in the White House's Oval Office, where so many famous men presided over history-making events. The presidential press secretary enters, a harried look on his rapidly aging face. He spills out the highlights of the latest wave of UFO sightings, wishing he were anywhere else, doing anything but this.

He launches into what is fast becoming a ritual about the Washington press corps (once his friends) hounding him for answers. The usual brush-off about UFOs being temperature inversions and weather balloons no longer works: They've heard too many reports of huge, windowless, metallic craft flying rings around our hottest fighter planes to fall for that any more. A few of the guys have come right out and called the press secretary a liar, and that hurts.

What do you—the president of the United States—do? Do you admit that you and your predecessors back to Harry Truman lied to the American people when you assured them there was no reality to UFOs? You might like to, but you know that once you concede even the remote possibility that UFOs are anything more than mistakes and imagination, you will have opened the floodgates to a million awkward questions that will demand answers you simply are not prepared to give.

Do you admit that there are unexplained vehicles flying through American skies, knowing you will then have to explain why you don't know whose they are? And why, after more than forty years, the world's greatest air force remains powerless to interfere in any way with their activities? Such an admission of impotence (and, by implication, ineptitude) in the face of what could easily be seen as a threat to national security, would cast into disrepute the entire American air defense system. This would not please the taxpayers, who remember shelling out tens of billions of dollars in the expectation that they would be protected from above.

You might admit that a few unexplained craft have overflown the country, while claiming they constitute more of a curiosity than a threat. But the simple admission that even a few UFOs exist could well pop the cork out of the bottle. The noisy, but so far ineffective, private UFO community has for decades been claiming UFOs were real. By conceding this single point to them, you would have raised their stature and quite possibly elevated them to the status of authorities on a subject sadly lacking in reliable sources of information. After years of bashing their heads against a stone wall erected by your own intelligence services, they might suddenly become experts whose opinions would be eagerly sought by TV network anchormen. And be responsible for even more gray hairs on the head of your press secretary.

And if there are confirmed Unidentified Flying Objects overhead, as the amateurs had long insisted and the government had just as long denied, couldn't the scarier claims of close-range sightings also be true? As long as those in authority—government leaders, scientists—agreed that not a single so-called UFO had ever been seen, such far-out concepts as UFO landings and alien abductions had seemed preposterous. But once the idea of genuine UFOs in the sky had been recognized, then it would be a short step to the acceptance of more direct approaches. After all, the government had admitted lying about the very existence of UFOs! Why assume any of its other denials were based on reality?

Of course, you, the president, could stick to the old party line and continue to insist there are no UFOs at all. Each time there has been a major flurry of sightings in the past, the press showed signs of losing confidence in official explanations. But then, after the furor died down, everything went back to the way it had been before. UFOs were forgotten by almost everyone, since nothing had resulted from their presence, just the way it would have been if they had never been here in the first place.

But there is a serious risk in making repeated denials in the face of a growing mass of evidence from more and more expert witnesses. If the public and/or the press ever decide the government has been dishonest in its handling of the UFO question, then all is lost. Nothing the president says will be believed, and even the most outlandish rumors may be accepted, in the absence of a dependable, official source of information that is responsive to the public need.

When the point is reached that the danger is not being believed exceeds the danger of the public learning what has really been going on, then it will be time to start releasing the truth about UFOs, no matter whose reputation is sullied in the process. With hundreds of people involved in the complex deception demanded by a massive cover-up, some of them will have to suffer when it all comes out into the open. As long as the president's aides can twist things around to make it look like he is on the side of truth and justice, the others will have to fend for themselves.

Then comes the problem of deciding when and how to release the information so long withheld. Do you simply dump it on the people and hope that it will be carefully sorted through and analyzed by thoughtful citizens who won't jump to conclusions? Or do you release it in carefully measured doses, observing the response of the "patient" to the "medicine" in order to determine what to do next? You are taking a very large risk that the release of the first bits of news will unleash a tidal wave of press curiosity that you will not be able to control.

If you tell the people that UFOs are (or even were) flying overhead, they may accept that and think no more of it. Or they may decide that if you are willing to admit that much, there must be more to it, and so they may be receptive to reports (authoritative or sensational) of landings, crashes, confrontations, and abductions. If you have the time, you may be able to conduct some tests of public reaction, releasing a small amount of relatively mild information to a limited audience and carefully monitoring the reactions. But if you are under pressure as a result of waiting until the last moment in hopes they will go away, this may not be possible and you'll just have to take your chances.

The real danger lies in the nature of the information you have been withholding. If it is fairly benign, then the risks are minimal. But if it is truly shocking, it may be worth almost any risk to keep it from becoming public knowledge.

The least upsetting possibility is that while UFOs may have been cruising through our skies for uncounted decades, they have never given any indication of being unfriendly, or of interacting with us. If that is the case, then the main risk is to Man's pride. Long accustomed to seeing himself as the ultimate example of power and knowledge, capable of overcoming any challenge to his stature, Man's realization that there are those flying right over our heads who have superior technology and are able to proceed with impunity could be a severe blow.

Since prehistoric times, Man has lorded it over the animals and over other men, and he has felt secure in his position at the top of the mountain. Alien craft—and, by implication, aliens, whether flying the UFOs the way pilots fly airplanes or operating them by remote control—would reduce Man to a position of subservience. But a novel form of subservience which has not yet produced any real changes in Man's behavior. No chains, no bowing down in their presence, no saluting an alien flag, no having to ask permission. Not even any restrictions on his precious freedoms of speech, assembly, or even thought.

Reactions to this shocking realization will be neither simple nor consistent. Some, who have long accepted that UFOs are real and probably alien, may take the news quite calmly, having had years to condition themselves. Others, who have long been aware of UFOs but never considered them of much interest because they were never personally touched, may shrug their shoulders and move along to the sports page. Still others, however, may find the news highly upsetting, especially if they have accepted the years of official denials as "proof" that UFOs cannot exist as anything different and important. Then the past will come back to haunt those who, for one reason or another, made authoritative-sounding statements discrediting UFOs, their observers and all those who found them interesting.

The most flamboyant proponents of UFO reality (saucer fans, New-Age believers, tabloid editors) will no doubt make certain that the world knows how far-sighted they were. This will add to the difficulty of keeping the public calm. But as long as UFOs are seen as having come no closer than a few thousand feet overhead, it should be possible to convince most people that nothing traumatic is about to happen.

But as UFOs come closer—or their closer approaches are confirmed by government agencies—the danger of strong public reaction will grow. Once it is admitted that they have had any sort of impact on people or the environment (what are called Close Encounters of the Second Kind and involve physiological and physical effects), it will be easy for any individual to visualize one of the spooky things bothering him. A UFO that can frighten one innocent driver on a lonely road at night by flying alongside and shining a bright light into his car can presumably do the same thing to others. Even if no real harm results, strong feelings of insecurity could engulf much of the population.

Even if the government doesn't confirm close approaches

and instances of interference, once overflights are accepted, it will require no great leap of the imagination to believe some of the more sensational claims that have been made over the years. And let's face it: If something can fly, it probably can land as well. And if it can land, then whoever was flying it so proficiently should be able to climb out and do who-knows-what. Visions of hideous, slobbering monsters from science fiction movies will trigger far too many imaginations, in the absence of calming facts.

While the information will spread more slowly by word of mouth, it will have a secondary effect of damaging the government's credibility as the public realizes that it is not being told the full story and that its leaders cannot be trusted. The public, for the most part, might still accept the staggering news and learn how to go about its business. Even if the weird idea of "alien abductions" becomes an accepted part of life, such experiences are brief and rarely produce long-term physical harm, and open discussion might reduce the psychological damage. But there would almost certainly be long-term effects on human culture.

First off, there is the world political and military situation. With the accelerating rush toward East–West peace, the addition of a third element, the aliens, may not have the great impact that it might have had in the days of the cold war. Military-related industries are preparing themselves for a major adjustment to civilian products and services, as military forces are being cut back. The recognition of aliens in our midst, or at least in our skies, could speed up the alliance of the long-antagonistic major powers. Ronald Reagan, when president, said on at least four occasions that a threat from outer space might unite the nations of Earth.

The most immediate and painful result of the widespread recognition of the presence of aliens would be the rapid drop in the value of defense shares on the stock market. It would be hard to see the long-term value of military aircraft, radar, ships, and missiles in the face of vastly superior technology that could probably be used to overwhelm Earth if that fit the aliens' plans. Why worry about threats from other countries when a much more ominous threat cruises right above us?

With the drop in the value of defense stocks would come similar drops in the value of stocks of hundreds of firms doing defense-related work, especially in research and development. A stock market crash of epic proportions is easy to envision, and would be followed by the layoff of hundreds of thousands of blue-collar and white-collar employees and the rapid failure of all sorts of service and support businesses. A deep depression could well follow in a very short time.

This alone could be keeping the U.S. government (in concert with others) from releasing the news of the existence and nature of UFOs. What president would want to go down in history as the space-age Herbert Hoover, with the blame for a financial catastrophe on his record? Of course, if the news could be let out slowly, so that the economy could adjust to the new demands a little at a time, then a deep crisis might be averted. But, as we have suggested, the chances of pacing the release of information may not be very good.

Even if the financial situation could be controlled, there are other elements in our culture that might not react as well. Religion, for example. How would the major organized religions react to the presence of aliens in our midst? No doubt many of them would immediately claim the aliens as their own, convinced that living, intelligent beings from anywhere must have come to the same conclusions on matters of philosophy and dogma as they had.

But what if the aliens practice a religion closely resembling one familiar religion and thus reject all the others? Or if they practice a religion bearing absolutely no similarity to any of Earth's major or minor religions, and thus reject all of ours? Or if their lives include nothing that bears the slightest resemblance to religion at all, and thus reject the very idea of religion and of a supreme being? For that matter, what if they had gone through a period of Earthlike religious behavior and then past it to a nonreligious life that clearly suited them better?

Would religious leaders accept this maturely, or would they

launch great drives to convince the aliens (and incidentally their straying flocks) of the absolute necessity of adopting their "one and only true" faith? Would they band together for a religious war on the aliens? While masses of chanting, swaying co-religionists jamming the centers of major cities might fit the needs of some church leaders who see their authority slipping away, the impact on religious tolerance could be devastating.

Regardless, the aliens' attitudes toward Earth religions would almost certainly be a very upsetting experience for hundreds of millions of people around the world who had been taught from childhood that theirs is the only true faith of the universe. If these obviously advanced beings function well without a recognizable deity, the need for religion as we know it would be diluted if not eliminated. The response of the major churches will tell the story, and experience does not suggest basis for optimism.

In the broad and increasingly important areas of science and technology, the realization that others are decades, centuries, or perhaps millennia ahead of us could be a blow to the collective ego from which we would never recover. So many of the world's best thinkers are involved in the systematic search for new and better ways of doing things that to destroy their motivation to do original work could be devastating.

The field most directly affected by the recognition that others had solved the major and minor problems of manned space flight would be the space programs of the United States, the former USSR, and the lesser nations in the space business. Pouring billions into sophisticated efforts to colonize the Moon and to explore Mars would suddenly appear as pointless as trying to build better dirt roads for Roman chariots. Cape Canaveral and the Russian space base at Tyuratam would quickly become museums instead of jumping-off places for Man's most exciting adventures.

And what of the thousands of highly educated and experienced specialists who had devoted their professional lives to the space programs? They would lose not only their jobs but their honored places in society as well. They would be as outdated as those who once made arrowheads by chipping flint. Also left without motivation would be hundreds of thousands of young people in many countries who had been inspired to study harder in hopes of one day joining their national space programs and perhaps doing important things for humanity.

The most technologically advanced cultures on Earth could shrink back toward an earlier, less sophisticated stage, as has been seen when a modern society inadvertently wipes out a primitive one. All this and more could be keeping the president from giving so much as a hint that UFOs are real. And hoping that the inevitable unexpected landing or crash in public will happen after he has retired to write his incomplete memoirs.

Stanton Friedman, a scientist, sees the future in a different way. His views follow.

The implications for mankind of aliens in the here and now will depend to a great extent on how they are presented. Either by themselves, in the middle of the World Series. Or by our own government finally admitting that "Oh, yeah, aliens have been coming here and we've known about it for more than forty years."

Portraying the aliens as evil could be a force for getting residents of this planet to work together. It could be a real boon for the defense industries, with Americans, Russians, Germans, Japanese, and so on all working together for the good of humankind. But if they are presented as good, it is conceivable that the space industries will boom. There could be movement toward colonizing other planets in our solar system, moving out toward the home base of the aliens, assuming it's in the "neighborhood."

Can they move us forward in space technology so that we, too, can go to the stars? Now, here's the big question: Will we go as visitors, as slaves, as equals or as possible students in some cosmic kindergarten? Will there be a space tourist business to make arrangements for visiting aliens who wish to go hunting or fishing, or even to have their equivalent of a honeymoon? What if it turns out that the aliens are coming here because they have discovered that there's a catastrophe in Earth's future? It could be an asteroid on a collision course. Or we could be approaching a region of space that has a high radiation level. Or we may be scheduled for destruction by a different alien race. The number of scenarios is limited only by the imagination. If we are facing a catastrophe, are they preparing to save some or all of us? Are they preparing to review our response? Will this be an incentive for us to be subservient to them? We just don't know.

What if it turns out that the aliens are really the gods of the Bible? That is, the all-powerful beings who have been here before, done their thing, left, and now come back to throw their technological hat into the ring? Suppose they had been here two thousand years ago and had subsequently traveled at almost the speed of light so that time slowed down for them while it went on for the people they left behind? They might be the same beings who were here in Jesus' time, and had left Jesus or other religious leaders behind and are now back to check on how things had gone. That sounds like science fiction, but when you recognize the Einsteinian relativity indicates that for people traveling at extremely high speed time slows down, then we have the startling possibility that we are an old experiment being evaluated. They may not be terribly impressed by the ways we've learned to kill each other, or our inability to meet many of the basic needs of so many people on our planet.

What if it turns out that there have been direct meetings between Earth's representatives and the aliens, and even exchange programs, for the past thirty years? There is a story about movie footage existing of a meeting at Holloman Air Force Base in the 1960s which could very well be true. If so. . . .

What if it turns out that we are somebody's private property? Certainly the residents of the Americas didn't have much say about conflicting territorial claims made by European explorers in the sixteenth and seventeenth centuries. In other words, our planet may be an area in dispute among several different groups of aliens. There is also the possibility that this was a prison colony, sort of a quarantine location, where they could dump undesirables and give them a chance at making it or failing.

It may also be that the reason for aliens coming here is purely economic. What do we have that might interest aliens? One thing might be biological material. It could be the DNA that belongs to people and of which we have many variations on the human theme—incredible variations of defects, strengths, weaknesses. And there is also plant and animal DNA, genetic structural material. We have an undifferentiated biological population with, for example, ten thousand varieties of sorghum. Whatever characteristics you want, there are probably a few seeds with those characteristics. The same holds for fish and mammals, many species and varieties of which have been around for a very long time. If, in the alien society, they have learned to control reproduction under laboratory conditions for people, animals, and plants, it may be that a new disease has arisen. It may be that they need certain characteristics because they want to explore places where their own biological make-up is inappropriate. One can imagine innumerable combinations of their genes and ours that might fit their specialized needs. We don't know.

It seems likely that any really advanced technological civilization will have studied biology as well as technology and may have learned the "secrets" of aging. That may have led them to a path around the aging problem. In other words, if there are certain biological clocks that need to be reset, if there are certain stimuli that are negative, these may have been placed under control so that an advanced civilization able to move between stars lives longer than we do.

Now, suppose aliens are the equivalent of three hundred human years old, have been taught using ultra-advanced computers, and have access to information developed by many different civilizations over a long period of time. This is very different from our situation—where all our knowledge was acquired in the last few thousand years, which is a brief time on a cosmic time scale. Under such conditions, one might expect some of the alien visitors to be extremely well educated. Their thinking may be very convoluted with regard to us, however. It may be that they have stood back and said that while many of us have the potential for good and are presumably educable, our leaders leave a great deal to be desired.

We (the aliens) got here in the 1940s because we detected growing technology. They (humans) had managed to kill forty million of their own in a great war, and destroyed much of their own planet. The next thing they did, rather than figure out how to live at peace with each other, was to develop competing groups with new weapons of great destructive capabilities and then let "great leaders" kill millions more of their own in their "enlightened self-interest."

This (Earth) is a society in serious trouble, as it seems to have developed mostly along the line of devising ever more efficient ways of killing its own. Do we want them to move out into space, or should they be kept on Earth?

In view of their own attitude toward life, they surely can't object to our doing a few biological experiments on them. We may have borrowed a few thousand of them, while they allow tens of thousands of children to die every day from preventable disease and starvation. How can they complain about what we do? Some of them insist we are cruel and "inhuman," yet they slaughter millions of animals every year for food and sport.

Another possibility is that the aliens are here for economic reasons that are entirely different from wanting valuable biological material. Earth is the densest planet in the solar system, containing very dense metals such as the little-known osmium and rhenium, along with platinum, uranium, and gold, some of which have very peculiar characteristics. Many of them have high melting points, high strength at high temperatures, and are very resistant to corrosion. Perhaps more important, they are quite rare in the universe, as we know from studying the spectra of stars.

Earth is therefore likely to have greater deposits of these

metals than any other planet in our own solar system, and possibly in the local neighborhood. The aliens may be staking out claims the way gold miners did in California and Alaska. They may even be staking out claims for materials we don't realize are important, just as prior to World War II we paid little attention to uranium, zirconium, and rare earths such as europium and neodymium. Now they are considered valuable metals, metals of commerce.

Earth could also be a laboratory for alien psychologists studying human behavior, much as we study rats in a maze, or monkeys under special conditions, using one-way mirrors and tape recorders. In view of our own difficulty in understanding ourselves, imagine how much more fascinating we may appear to aliens. Some of the most peculiar behavior of UFOs (a disc flying with its broad side forward, for example, or flipping end-over-end) could be analogous to a professor shocking his psychology class with some seemingly irrational act just to see how they will react.

It may be ego-satisfying to think that aliens visiting Earth must have some superspecial purpose, since their journey had to have been exceptionally difficult, dangerous, and long. But that would be as foolish as judging modern transatlantic flights by Charles Lindbergh's historic solo trip in 1927. From one brave man flying for thirty-four hours in a poorly equipped and hard-to-fly single-seater, we now have ten million people flying every year across the Atlantic in just six or seven hours. Many go for reasons which once would have been considered trivial but are perfectly acceptable because the trip is now so easy. If it took six months to get there, you wouldn't go to London for a weekend.

If aliens have been flying between stars for scores of generations or for millions of years, they could have as many reasons for coming to Earth as we have for going to New York City: good ones, bad ones, indifferent ones; personal ones, very public ones; immediate ones and long-term ones; happy ones and sad ones. Instead of trying to figure out what single purpose motivates aliens to visit here, perhaps we should be considering a wide range of concurrent possibilities.

As for the reason or reasons our own governments continue to insist they are not here at all, maybe they know something so upsetting that our knowing it won't help. Maybe something awful is happening, or is soon to happen, or could happen someday, and the prospect could disturb our way of life without helping to improve the situation. Even a hint of impending tragedy could be enough to cause a major uproar.

It is also possible that, just as Moses was kept out of the Promised Land because he was of the older generation that knew slavery, our governments could be waiting until all the old, narrow-minded military leaders have died, or at least retired. Max Planck, the great German physicist, said, "New ideas come to be accepted not because their opponents come to believe in them, but because their opponents die and a new generation grows up that is accustomed to them."

For the first time in history, we have a new generation that has never known a time when there wasn't a manned space program. Saturday-morning cartoons, television series like *Star Trek*, movies, and the evening news have combined to "brainwash" young people into space-consciousness.

Why are the aliens here? Where are they from? What, if anything, are their plans for us? Why haven't they presented themselves formally, rather than remaining as inconspicuous as possible? Why are governments determined to keep their presence secret? Lacking any knowledge of the aliens' psyches, we have no way to delve into their behavior. And lacking any entree to the most secret rooms in the Pentagon, we have no way to delve into the behavior of our own people vis-à-vis the aliens.

For almost a half-century of intense UFO activity in our atmosphere and on our ground, the data have piled up, as have the theories. But despite the efforts put into trying to solve the great mystery of the twentieth century, we may be no closer today then we were when UFOs crashed in the open spaces of New Mexico and the government easily fooled us all into thinking it was part of a weather balloon.

Conclusion

TWO VERY STRANGE devices crashed in central New Mexico in July 1947. They were not weather balloons, or test rockets, or secret military airplanes. By every indication, what crashed were two alien spacecraft, along with their crews of small humanoids.

Dozens of firsthand and secondhand witnesses have attested to the details of the crashes, to the retrievals of wreckage and bodies by the military, to their shipment out of New Mexico aboard military aircraft, and to the thorough and continuing cover-up by the U.S. government of perhaps the most important event in the past thousand years.

Except for a few hours on July 8, the story remained completely hidden for more than thirty years, thanks to an unusually effective job of government disinformation. It began to emerge only in 1978 when one of the first two military men to reach the scene of the Corona crash told his story to one of the authors. Slowly, more witnesses were found and added their testimony, enabling a more complete picture to be assembled.

Hundreds and possibly thousands of men and women have been involved in the huge, costly official effort to cope with the crashes, to transport, examine, and store wreckage and bodies and house at least one live alien, to learn who and what was involved and to keep it all secret. Those who initiated this process are long gone, and most of the others have successfully maintained their anonymity. But more and more public-spirited citizens are coming forth with new bits of information to help clarify this very complex matter.

Had it been generally realized back in 1947 that two vehicles from another advanced civilization had smashed into the New Mexico desert, mankind's modern history would certainly have been changed. As it is, that history has been walled up within the Pentagon and in various intelligence agencies where a select few know of it. The people of the world have been kept ignorant of a pair of events of incalculable proportions.

The U.S. government continues to insist that nothing of importance happened at Corona or San Agustin; that, in fact, nothing *at all* happened there! Its ability to maintain this position in the face of a growing collection of testimony from those who were there cannot survive forever.

A great deal has been accomplished by the authors and by others who have dedicated much of their lives to the search for the truth about the New Mexico events. But much remains to be done before those in high positions realize they have a moral duty to the American people to tell them what really happened almost two generations ago. The cold war is over. In a free society how can a free people make reasonable choices in ignorance?

Although we are racing the undertaker, the search for more and better evidence continues. If you had any involvement with the New Mexico crashes please get in touch with the authors. If you know of anyone else who was involved, let us know. Witness names will not be used without permission. And if you have information about any other crashes of UFOs, in the United States or elsewhere, we need your help. Call or write: Stanton Friedman, P.O. Box 958, Houlton, Maine 04730; telephone (506) 457-0232 (call collect station-to-station any time). Or contact Don Berliner, #227, 1202 S. Washington Street, Alexandria, Virginia 22314; telephone (703) 548-0405.

Appendices

The Majestic-12 documents as received by Jaime Shandera in 1984.

A-1

TOP SECRET / MAJIC   0 0 1

EYES ONLY
NATIONAL SECURITY INFORMATION

•••••••••••••••
• TOP SECRET •
•••••••••••••••

EYES ONLY   COPY ONE OF ONE.

BRIEFING DOCUMENT: OPERATION MAJESTIC 12

PREPARED FOR PRESIDENT-ELECT DWIGHT D. EISENHOWER: (EYES ONLY)

18 NOVEMBER, 1952

WARNING! This is a TOP SECRET - EYES ONLY document containing
compartmentalized information essential to the national security
of the United States. EYES ONLY ACCESS to the material herein
is strictly limited to those possessing Majestic-12 clearance
level. Reproduction in any form or the taking of written or
mechanically transcribed notes is strictly forbidden.

•••••••••••••••
• TOP SECRET •
TOP SECRET / MAJIC   T52-EXEMPT (E)
EYES ONLY   EYES ONLY   0 0 1

COPY <u>ONE</u> OF <u>ONE</u>.

SUBJECT: OPERATION MAJESTIC-12 PRELIMINARY BRIEFING FOR
PRESIDENT-ELECT EISENHOWER.

DOCUMENT PREPARED 18 NOVEMBER, 1952.

BRIEFING OFFICER: ADM. ROSCOE H. HILLENKOETTER (MJ-1)

NOTE: This document has been prepared as a preliminary briefing
only. It should be regarded as introductory to a full operations
briefing intended to follow.

* * * * * *

OPERATION MAJESTIC-12 is a TOP SECRET Research and Development/
Intelligence operation responsible directly and only to the
President of the United States. Operations of the project are
carried out under control of the Majestic-12 (Majic-12) Group
which was established by special classified executive order of
President Truman on 24 September, 1947, upon recommendation by
Dr. Vannevar Bush and Secretary James Forrestal. (See Attachment
"A".) Members of the Majestic-12 Group were designated as follows:

Adm. Roscoe H. Hillenkoetter
Dr. Vannevar Bush
Secy. James V. Forrestal*
Gen. Nathan F. Twining
Gen. Hoyt S. Vandenberg
Dr. Detlev Bronk
Dr. Jerome Hunsaker
Mr. Sidney W. Souers
Mr. Gordon Gray
Dr. Donald Menzel
Gen. Robert M. Montague
Dr. Lloyd V. Berkner

The death of Secretary Forrestal on 22 May, 1949, created
a vacancy which remained unfilled until 01 August, 1950, upon
which date Gen. Walter B. Smith was designated as permanent
replacement.

* TOP SECRET *

TOP SECRET / MAJIC

EYES ONLY

EYES ONLY

T52-EXEMPT (E)

002

* TOP SECRET *
****

On 24 June, 1947, a civilian pilot flying over the Cascade
Mountains in the State of Washington observed nine flying
disc-shaped aircraft traveling in formation at a high rate
of speed. Although this was not the first known sighting
of such objects, it was the first to gain widespread attention
in the public media. Hundreds of reports of sightings of
similar objects followed. Many of these came from highly
credible military and civilian sources. These reports resulted in independent efforts by several different elements
of the military to ascertain the nature and purpose of these
objects in the interests of national defense. A number of
witnesses were interviewed and there were several unsuccessful
attempts to utilize aircraft in efforts to pursue reported
discs in flight. Public reaction bordered on near hysteria
at times.

In spite of these efforts, little of substance was learned
about the objects until a local rancher reported that one
had crashed in a remote region of New Mexico located approximately seventy-five miles northwest of Roswell Army Air
Base (now Walker Field).

On 07 July, 1947, a secret operation was begun to assure
recovery of the wreckage of this object for scientific study.
During the course of this operation, aerial reconnaissance
discovered that four small human-like beings had apparently
ejected from the craft at some point before it exploded.
These had fallen to earth about two miles east of the wreckage
site. All four were dead and badly decomposed due to action
by predators and exposure to the elements during the approximately one week time period which had elapsed before their
discovery. A special scientific team took charge of removing
these bodies for study. (See Attachment "C".) The wreckage
of the craft was also removed to several different locations.
(See Attachment "B".) Civilian and military witnesses in
the area were debriefed, and news reporters were given the
effective cover story that the object had been a misguided
weather research balloon.

****
* TOP SECRET *
****

<u>EYES ONLY</u>

A covert analytical effort organized by Gen. Twining and
Dr. Bush acting on the direct orders of the President, resulted in a preliminary concensus (19 September, 1947) that
the disc was most likely a short range reconnaissance craft.
This conclusion was based for the most part on the craft's
size and the apparent lack of any identifiable provisioning.
(See Attachment "D".) A similar analysis of the four dead
occupants was arranged by Dr. Bronk. It was the tentative
conclusion of this group (30 November, 1947) that although
these creatures are human-like in appearance, the biological
and evolutionary processes responsible for their development
has apparently been quite different from those observed or
postulated in homo-sapiens. Dr. Bronk's team has suggested
the term "Extra-terrestrial Biological Entities", or "EBEs",
be adopted as the standard term of reference for these
creatures until such time as a more definitive designation
can be agreed upon.

Since it is virtually certain that these craft do not originate in any country on earth, considerable speculation has
centered around what their point of origin might be and how
they get here. Mars was and remains a possibility, although
some scientists, most notably Dr. Menzel, consider it more
likely that we are dealing with beings from another solar
system entirely.

Numerous examples of what appear to be a form of writing
were found in the wreckage. Efforts to decipher these have
remained largely unsuccessful. (See Attachment "E".)
Equally unsuccessful have been efforts to determine the
method of propulsion or the nature or method of transmission
of the power source involved. Research along these lines
has been complicated by the complete absence of identifiable
wings, propellers, jets, or other conventional methods of
propulsion and guidance, as well as a total lack of metallic
wiring, vacuum tubes, or similar recognizable electronic
components. (See Attachment "F".) It is assumed that the
propulsion unit was completely destroyed by the explosion
which caused the crash.

COPY ONE OF ONE.

A need for as much additional information as possible about
these craft, their performance characteristics and their
purpose led to the undertaking known as U.S. Air Force Project
SIGN in December, 1947. In order to preserve security, liason
between SIGN and Majestic-12 was limited to two individuals
within the Intelligence Division of Air Materiel Command whose
role was to pass along certain types of information through
channels. SIGN evolved into Project GRUDGE in December, 1948.
The operation is currently being conducted under the code name
BLUE BOOK, with liason maintained through the Air Force officer
who is head of the project.

On 06 December, 1950, a second object, probably of similar
origin, impacted the earth at high speed in the El Indio –
Guerrero area of the Texas – Mexican boder after following
a long trajectory through the atmosphere. By the time a
search team arrived, what remained of the object had been almost
totally incinerated. Such material as could be recovered was
transported to the A.E.C. facility at Sandia, New Mexico, for
study.

Implications for the National Security are of continuing importance in that the motives and ultimate intentions of these
visitors remain completely unknown. In addition, a significant
upsurge in the surveillance activity of these craft beginning
in May and continuing through the autumn of this year has caused
considerable concern that new developments may be imminent.
It is for these reasons, as well as the obvious international
and technological considerations and the ultimate need to
avoid a public panic at all costs, that the Majestic-12 Group
remains of the unanimous opinion that imposition of the
strictest security precautions should continue without inter-
ruption into the new administration. At the same time, contingency plan MJ-1949-04P/78 (Top Secret - Eyes Only) should
he held in continued readiness should the need to make a
public announcement present itself. (See Attachment "G".)

```
. . . . . . . . . . . . . .
*  TOP SECRET  *
. . . . . . . . . . . . . .
```

<u>EYES ONLY</u>   COPY <u>ONE</u> OF <u>ONE</u>.

ENUMERATION OF ATTACHMENTS:

•ATTACHMENT "A".......Special Classified Executive
                     Order #092447. (TS/EO)

•ATTACHMENT "B".......Operation Majestic-12 Status
                     Report #1, Part A. 30 NOV '47.
                     (TS-MAJIC/EO)

•ATTACHMENT "C".......Operation Majestic-12 Status
                     Report #1, Part B. 30 NOV '47.
                     (TS-MAJIC/EO)

•ATTACHMENT "D".......Operation Majestic-12 Preliminary
                     Analytical Report. 19 SEP '47.
                     (TS-MAJIC/EO)

•ATTACHMENT "E".......Operation Majestic-12 Blue Team
                     Report #5. 30 JUN '52.
                     (TS-MAJIC/EO)

•ATTACHMENT "F".......Operation Majestic-12 Status
                     Report #2. 31 JAN '48.
                     (TS-MAJIC/EO)

•ATTACHMENT "G".......Operation Majestic-12 Contingency
                     Plan MJ-1949-04P/78: 31 JAN '49.
                     (TS-MAJIC/EO)

•ATTACHMENT "H".......Operation Majestic-12, Maps and
                     Photographs Folio (Extractions).
                     (TS-MAJIC/EO)

```
. . . . . . . . . . . . . .
*  TOP SECRET  *
```
TOP SECRET / MAJIC
<u>EYES ONLY</u>   ## EYES ONLY   T52-EXEMPT (E)
                                                      006

```
* * * * * * * * * * * * *
* TOP SECRET *
* * * * * * * * * * * * *
```

EYES ONLY

COPY ONE OF ONE.

ATTACHMENT "A"

```
* * * * * * * * * * * * *
* TOP SECRET *
* * * * * * * * * * * * *
```

September 24, 1947.

MEMORANDUM FOR THE SECRETARY OF DEFENSE

Dear Secretary Forrestal:

    As per our recent conversation on this matter, you are hereby authorized to proceed with all due speed and caution upon your undertaking. Hereafter this matter shall be referred to only as Operation Majestic Twelve.

    It continues to be my feeling that any future considerations relative to the ultimate disposition of this matter should rest solely with the Office of the President following appropriate discussions with yourself, Dr. Bush and the Director of Central Intelligence.

Harry Truman

Notes by S.T. Friedman: This document was found after a few days of searching in the just
declassified boxes of Record Group 341 in Mid 1985 by Jaime Shandera and William Moore.
Stanton Friedman had discovered during a visit to the National Archives in March 1985
that the RG was in the process of being classification reviewed. Post cards were received
hinting that checking the file would be a good idea. This memo clearly has nothing to do
with anything else in Box 189 where it was found. Most likely it was planted there during
the classification review which involved many teams of 4 each working for a few weeks in
a location where they were able to bring in notes, files, brief cases etc.The item in its
original form is a carbon on Dictation Onion Skin by Fox Paper. It is discolored
around the edges. My best bet for the actual   July 14, 1954
author is James S. Lay who was Exec. Sec of NSC
and worked very very closely with Cutler and met
"off the Record" with Ike at the WH on July 14, 1954.   TOP SECRET RESTRICTED
The mark through the classification is red ⟶   SECURITY INFORMATION

MEMORANDUM FOR GENERAL TWINING

SUBJECT: NSC/MJ-12 Special Studies Project

     The President has decided that the MJ-12 SSP briefing
should take place during the already scheduled White House
meeting of July 16, rather than following it as previously
intended. More precise arrangements will be explained to
you upon arrival. Please alter your plans accordingly.

     Your concurrence in the above change of arrangements
is assumed.

Note that the last sentence is almost identical to the wording of another TS Cutler-Twining
memo found at the Library of Congress in the Twining papers.

                    ROBERT CUTLER
                    Special Assistant
                    to the President
          Note that there is no signature and no /s/

JND 857013
4/12/87

9. (TS) NSA-originated reports – Thirty-eight documents are the direct product of NSA SIGINT operations and one document describes classified SIGINT activities. These documents can be further described as follows:

a. The document describing SIGINT operations reports

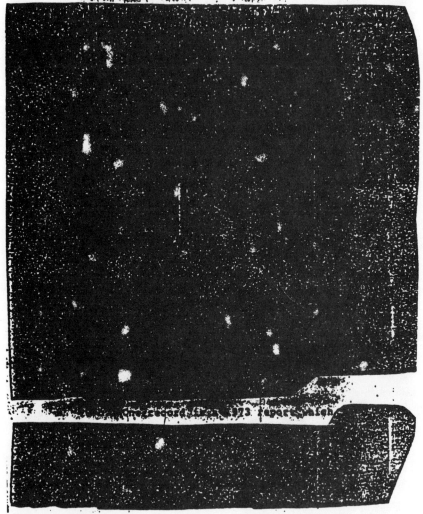

A typical page of a 21–page affidavit from the National Security Agency to a federal court judge justifying withholding one hundred and fifty six classified NSA UFO documents, as received by Stanton Friedman under a 1979 Freedom of Information Act request.

Suggested Reading

THE FIRST STEP, and often the biggest obstacle, for those wishing to learn more about UFOs is obtaining information that can be trusted. A good deal of the most up-to-date and reliable information is published at conferences or in UFO journals with very limited distribution, whereas much of the material that is widely available, whether in supermarket tabloids, on computer information systems, or in mass-circulation newspapers and magazines, is often of dubious reliability. The following is a list of some of the books, reports, films, and organizations that should be consulted to learn more about crashed saucers and UFOs in general.

Books

Berlitz, Charles, and Moore, William L., *The Roswell Incident.* New York: Grosset and Dunlop, 1980. 184 pages. Paperback edition by Berkley Books, 1988 ($3.95). Contains the first interviews with many of the key players of the events in New Mexico, but also includes a good deal of sensationalized, extraneous material.

Randle, Kevin, and Donald R. Schmitt. *UFO Crash at Roswell*, New York: Avon, 1991. 327 pages ($4.95). A considerable effort went into locating new witnesses, but the book, without a solid basis, discounts Gerald Anderson, moves the Barney Barnett story to near Corona, and casually dismisses the MJ-12 documents.

Weiner, Tim, *Blank Check: The Pentagon's Black Budget.* New

York: Warner Books, 1990. 273 pages ($21.95). Weiner, who has two Pulitzer Prizes for investigative journalism, does an excellent job of documenting the Pentagon's annual $34 billion "black budget" (research funds not under congressional control or review).

Reports and Other Publications

Eberhardt, George, ed., "The Roswell Report: An Historical Perspective." 1991, J. Allen Hynek Center for UFO Studies, 2457 W. Peterson Avenue, Chicago, Illinois, 60659. 145 pages, 8½" × 11" ($15). Includes twenty articles, of which twelve are reprints. Rebuttals to the major negative MJ-12 article are not included or referenced. Several new pieces, including one about Gerald Anderson, have numerous errors.

Friedman, Stanton T., "Flying Saucers, Noisy Negativists and Truth." MUFON Conference Paper, July 1985. Notes more than twenty misstatements by Phil Klass in his 3-page commentary about Roswell in one of his books. 17 pages, 15 references ($4 postpaid from UFO Research Institute, P.O. Box 958, Houlton, Maine 04730).

Friedman, Stanton T., "The Final Report on Operation Majestic 12." 1990, published and funded by the Fund for UFO Research, P.O. Box 277, Mt. Rainier, MD 20712 ($12.50) Also available from UFORI ($14 postpaid). 108 pages, 65 of text and many documents, correspondence with Phil Klass, copy of his check for $1000 for being proven wrong about the Cutler Twining Memo; debunks many anti-MJ-12 arguments. Lists thirty-three details in the documents not known earlier.

Friedman, Stanton T., "UFOs: Earth's Cosmic Watergate." 1981. The big picture of the UFO Cover-up, quotes from numerous government documents including instructions from USAF-OSI to all units to violate their own rules if an FOIA request is made to them concerning UFOs by S. T. Friedman. 22 pages ($4 postpaid from UFORI.)

Friedman, Stanton T., "Update on Crashed Saucers in New Mexico." Paper presented at the 22nd Annual MUFON International Symposium, Chicago, July, 1991. 20 pages, 8½" × 11" ($4 postpaid from UFORI). Entire conference proceedings available. 301 pages. (MUFON, 103 Oldtowne Road, Sequin, Texas, 78155. $20 + $1.50 for postage and handling).

Friedman, Stanton T., "Update on Operation Majestic 12." July 1989. Paper presented at MUFON International UFO Symposium, July 1989. Includes detailed data regarding MJ-12 members. 19 pages ($4 postpaid from UFORI).

Moore, W. L., "Crashed Saucers: Evidence in Search of Proof." Presented at the 1985 MUFON Symposium, St. Louis, Missouri, June, 1985. This is the best summary of the early work done by Friedman and Moore and also deals in depth with Frank Scully's 1950 book *Behind the Flying Saucers*. Available as a separate 49-page report from UFORI ($8 postpaid).

Moore, W. L. and Shandera, Jaime, "The MJ-12 Documents: an Analytical Report." 1990. Among the many details provided are specifics about type faces, styles, signatures, and various document disinformation efforts. Focuses on forensics. 111 pages, typeset, large format ($25 + $5 for first class postage from The Fair Witness Project, 4219 W. Olive Avenue, #247, Burbank, California, 91505).

Schmitt, Donald R., "New Revelations from Roswell." Presented at the MUFON Symposium, Pensacola, Florida, July, 1990. Proceedings pp. 154–168. Full volume 201 pages ($15 postpaid, from MUFON).

Stringfield, Leonard, "UFO Crash Retrievals—The Inner Sanctum." July, 1991. 142 pages ($17 + $1.50 postage & handling, from MUFON).

Articles

Carpenter, John S. "Gerald Anderson: Truth vs. Fiction." *MUFON UFO Journal*, No. 281 (Sept. 1991): 3–7, 12. Detailed critique of attacks against Gerald Anderson in "Roswell Report."

Friedman, Stanton T. "The MJ-12 Debunking Fiasco." *International UFO Reporter*, 13:3 (May/June 1988). Debunks many of the anti-MJ-12 claims of Phil Klass as published in *The Skeptical Inquirer*.

Friedman, Stanton T. "The Secret Life of Donald H. Menzel." *International UFO Reporter* (Jan./Feb. 1988): 20–24. Documents in detail the proof of Donald Menzel's double life as a UFO debunker and Harvard professor of Astronomy *and* effective employee of government agencies such as the NSA, the CIA, and the Navy (and very likely an important member of Operation Majestic 12).

Films

UFOS Are Real, 93-minute documentary movie which includes, among other features, the first interview with Jesse A. Marcel, Sr., interviews with four Ph.D.s, three Lt. Colonels, two abductees, Ted Phillips on physical trace cases, and many more UFO pictures. S. T. Friedman was co-script writer and technical advisor, on location and in the film ($45 postpaid from UFORI).

Whiting, Fred, *Reflections on Roswell*, 1992. 105-minute video with interviews of many of the most important crashed saucer witnesses. Available only from the Fund for UFO Research ($50).

Organizations

For general information about UFOs, send a self-addressed, stamped No. 10 size envelope to:

1) The Mutual UFO Network (MUFON), 103 Oldtowne Road, Seguin, Texas, 78155. Publishes the monthly *MUFON Journal* ($25 per year) and *Proceedings of the Annual MUFON International Symposium*, usually in July, as well as special reports. Has over 3,000 subscribers and numerous local units responsible for investigating cases in their area.

2) J. Allen Hynek Center for UFO Studies, 2457 Peterson Ave-

nue, Chicago, Illinois, 60659. Publishes bimonthly *International UFO Reporter* ($25 per year).

3) Fund for UFO Research, P.O. Box 277, Mt. Rainier, Maryland, 20712. NOT a membership organization. Has a distinguished Board of Directors and has raised more than $250,000 to support UFO-related research projects, with more than $50,000 spent on crashed saucer activities. Has a list of publications available, including declassified government documents. Contributions are tax deductible.

4) UFO Newsclipping Service, Route 1, Box 220, Plumerville, Arizona, 72127. At least twenty legal-size pages of UFO and Fortean clippings ($6 per month).

5) Arcturus Press, P.O. Box 831383, Stone Mountain, Georgia, 30083. Specializes in UFO publications including used copies of old classics.

6) *UFO Magazine*, 1536 S. Robertson Blvd., Los Angeles, California, 90035. Bimonthly ($21 per year).

7) Omega Communications, P.O. Box 2051, Cheshire, Connecticut, 06410. Produces an annual conference, "The UFO Experience," and records the proceedings on audio and video tape. Has a list of dozens of illustrated lectures by leading UFO investigators, including Stanton Friedman and Don Berliner, plus UFO contactees and abductees.

UFOLINE provides information about various aspects of the UFO phenomenon. Information is provided by Stanton Friedman. 1–900–446–UFOS (8367). Calls are $2 for the first minute; $1 per minute thereafter. Messages and sighting reports can be left.

Index